The Road Goes Ever On

Copyright © 2022 by A. K. Frailey.

All rights reserved. No part of this book may be used or reproduced by any means, graphic, electronic, or mechanical, including photocopying, recording, taping or by any information storage retrieval system without the written permission of the publisher.

A. K. Frailey Books
110 Possum Lane
Fillmore, IL 62032

Cover and Interior: Trese Gloriod
Cover Photo: Adobe Stock

Second Edition

ISBN: 979-8-9861803-0-4

A. K. FRAILEY

The ROAD GOES EVER ON

A Christian Journey Through The Lord of the Rings

Second Edition
A. K. Frailey Books
Fillmore, Illinois

The Writings of A. K. Frailey

Books for the Mind and Spirit
https://akfrailey.com/
Contact: akfrailey@yahoo.com

Historical Science Fiction Novels
OldEarth ARAM Encounter https://amzn.to/2KLhlsN
OldEarth Ishtar Encounter https://amzn.to/2OAkDQF
OldEarth Neb Encounter https://amzn.to/3iGqGlQ
OldEarth Georgios Encounter https://amzn.to/3v7w8oI
OldEarth Melchior Encounter https://amzn.to/3nyfkEJ

Science Fiction Novels
Homestead https://amzn.to/3DcTuhz
Last of Her Kind http://amzn.to/2y1HJvg
Newearth Justine Awakens http://amzn.to/2pq0vWN
Newearth A Hero's Crime https://amzn.to/3S4rROI

Short Stories
***It Might Have Been—And Other Short Stories* 2nd Edition**
https://amzn.to/2XXdDDz
One Day at a Time and Other Stories https://amzn.to/2YFtQ5r
***Encounter Science Fiction Short Stories & Novella* 2nd Edition**
https://amzn.to/3dq6q5l

Inspirational Non-Fiction
***My Road Goes Ever On—Spiritual Being, Human Journey* 2nd Edition**
https://amzn.to/2KvF3Ll
My Road Goes Ever On—A Timeless Journey https://amzn.to/3v5BlOM
The Road Goes Ever On—A Christian Journey Through The Lord of the Rings
https://amzn.to/3rtAy6S

Children's Book
The Adventures of Tally-Ho http://amzn.to/2sLfcI5

Poetry
***Hope's Embrace & Other Poems* 2nd Edition** https://amzn.to/3cn22X8

Diocese of Springfield in Illinois
Catholic Pastoral Center • 1615 West Washington Street • P.O. Box 3187 • Springfield, Illinois 62708-3187
www.dio.org   217-698-8500   FAX 217-698-0802

Office of the Bishop

IMPRIMATUR

The designated diocesan censor has reviewed *Christian Themes in the Lord of the Rings* by Ann Frailey and has found the contents to be free of doctrinal and moral error. Therefore, I decree that it may be published in accordance with the requirements of canon 824 of the Code of Canon Law.

The following text must be printed in the book:

Nihil Obstat
Very Reverend Kevin M. Laughery, JCL
Judicial Vicar
Diocese of Springfield in Illinois
October 18, 2010

Imprimatur
Most Reverend Thomas John Paprocki
Bishop of Springfield in Illinois
November 1, 2010

The *Nihil Obstat* and *Imprimatur* are declarations that the material is free from doctrinal or moral error, and thus is granted permission to publish in accordance with c. 827. No legal responsibility is assumed by the grant of this permission. No implication is contained herein that those who have granted the *Nihil Obstat* and *Imprimatur* agree with the content, opinions, or statements expressed.

It is understood that Mrs. Ann Frailey, of the Diocese of Springfield in Illinois, will self-publish this work using an online publishing service. After publication, two copies of this work are to be sent to the Archivist for the Diocese of Springfield in Illinois for placement in the Diocesan Archives.

† Thomas John Paprocki
Most Reverend Thomas John Paprocki
Bishop of Springfield in Illinois

Cheryl A. Kannall
Mrs. Cheryl Kannall
Ecclesiastical Notary

November 1, 2010
Springfield, Illinois

We read literature because we find truth in it. We would not find imaginative stories compelling if their made-up situations were in no way related to life as we experience it. Literature in fact holds up a mirror to human beings. We frequently find that persons and societies supposedly far removed from us tell the truth about things we observe in the intimacy of our own hearts.

What could be more far removed from us than the literary works described as "fantasy"? This very name denotes worlds which are not our world. The author invents creatures and worlds which we do not encounter except in the pages of a book. Are we to find truth in fantasy?

The answer is yes, particularly when the author is J. R. R. Tolkien. He invites us to Middle-earth with its strange beings, some resembling human beings as we know them, some bearing an approximation of human form, and some not looking at all like us. But we are to look within the minds of these creatures and see enacted the same kind of drama that goes on in each of us – a true struggle between good and evil.

Ann Frailey has seen very clearly the human drama portrayed in the events of Tolkien's trilogy about the ring of power. She guides us through a strange land and helps us to identify with the strangeness to be found in our hearts as we navigate our own course through life. There are conquests open for each of us. We come to understand that there is a way for us to find strength, and the way leads through and acknowledgment of weakness and our absolute need for God. Expect to be encouraged in your own quest for meaning.

Father Kevin Laughery
Catholic Diocese of Springfield in Illinois

Acknowledgements

Thank you to the Author of all goodness and His many faithful friends: Father Kevin Laughery, Most Reverend Thomas John Paprocki, Mrs. Cheryl Kannall, John LaBriola, and Lu Cortese. I owe a debt of gratitude to my very supportive family: my late husband John, and all my children, Ian, William, Kristin, Teresa, Laura, Rebekah, Daniel, and Elizabeth. For all that is good, true and beautiful, I thank God.

Table of Contents

Introduction.. 1

Chapter One
What Makes Our Heroes So Heroic?..................... 5
    Faith... 5
    Hope.. 10
    Charity... 15

Chapter Two
Warriors Awake!.. 22
    Prudence.. 23
    Justice... 27
    Fortitude.. 33
    Temperance.. 37

Chapter Three
Gifts From On High.. 43
    Wisdom.. 45
    Understanding..................................... 48
    Counsel... 50
    Fortitude.. 54
    Knowledge.. 58
    Piety... 61
    Fear of the Lord................................... 64

Chapter Four
The Rings of Power 67
    Pride 72
    Covetousness 76
    Lust 81
    Anger 87
    Gluttony 91
    Envy 95
    Sloth 99

Chapter Five
Lead Us Not Into Temptation 104
    Computers and Television 107
    Medical Technology 112
    Communication Systems 117

Chapter Six
Our Heroes and Saints 120
    Frodo and Saint Thomas More 122
    Sam and Saint Isidore the Farmer 125
    Pippin and Merry and St. Tarsicius 128
    Gandalf and Moses 132
    Gimli and Saint Patrick 136
    Legolas and Saint John the Apostle 140
    Boromir and Saint Augustine 143
    Faramir and Saint Thomas Aquinas 149
    Eowyn and Saint Clare 153
    Galadriel and the Communion of Saints 159
    Aragorn and the Hidden King 163

Chapter Seven
Summary 168

Introduction

"But in the wearing of the swift years of Middle-earth the line of Meneldil son of Anarion failed, and the tree withered, and the blood of the Numenoreans became mingled with that of lesser men. Then the watch upon the walls of Mordor slept, and dark things crept back to Gorgoroth. And on a time evil things came forth, and they took Minas Ithil and abode in it, and they made it into a place of dread;..." (The Fellowship of the Ring)

The first time I read of Hobbits and their adventures I was eleven years old and I was borrowing *The Hobbit* from a friend. When it came to the dark mines of the goblins I was unnerved, and I could not finish the story. I felt as if I had missed something of importance but what it was I could not at that time discern.

When I was much older, carrying my second child, and enduring the torments of severe morning sickness, my husband suggested I read *The Lord of the Rings* to get my mind off my suffering. It was a strange suggestion as I think of it now, but it turned out to be a wonderful act of benevolent insight if ever there was one. I began *The Hobbit* again, to get the background, and I felt myself drawn into a world that spoke volumes to a heart that was expanding as it never had before.

In that reading, and in subsequent readings, I glimpsed the mind of a soul that saw meaning in the lives of the most varied characters which reflect the real world people in our own lives.

Even more surprisingly, there are reflections of the various aspects of each of our own personalities.

The story of *The Hobbit* and the continuing adventure, *The Lord of the Rings*, speaks to many universal themes. As Tolkien was a Catholic, he surely reflected the teaching and thoughts of the moral forces around him. He lived through two great world wars and undoubtedly saw in his teaching profession and marriage, as well as in fatherhood, both the noble and the treacherous parts of our human experience as we struggle to overcome temptations and become transformed into the beings God called us forth to be from the beginning of time. As he himself said while talking with C.S. Lewis one night; "We have come from God, and inevitably the myths woven by us, though they contain error, will also reflect a splintered fragment of the true light, the eternal truth that is with God. Indeed only by myth-making, only by becoming a 'sub-creator' and inventing stories, can man aspire to the state of perfection that he knew before the fall. Our myths may be misguided, but they steer however shakily toward the true harbor, while materialistic 'progress' leads only to a yawning abyss and the Iron Crown of the power of evil." (J.R.R. Tolkien: A biography, by Humphrey Carpenter, page 151)

In each character in *The Lord of the Rings,* it is as if we can see the various struggles each person on this Earth must grapple with in order to advance to that state of perfection which our Lord calls us to as sons and daughters of God. It is in the development or the abandonment of the practice of Christian virtues that each character either ascends into greatness or descends into madness and evil. In the prudent justice of Bilbo, the wise fortitude of Frodo, and the faithful hope of Sam, so each of us is called to reflect on our own lives; the virtues we practice or ignore, and the meaning of our existence.

We can see so clearly in the movie depiction the glory and wonder of the adventure as it is played out so magnificently in bright images on a large screen. Then it seems that the ordinary becomes truly extraordinary and meaningless acts of mere living suddenly take on a value of tremendous proportions. If we look at the story and those same characters through the lens of faith in the one true and perfect God, then we would find that our own existence can be revealed for the wonder that it is. For everything we do has meaning and though we may never have a song sung about us and we may never have our personal memoirs published, that does not in any way diminish the nobility of our struggle to become what we are called to be. If anything, it is suggested by our Lord Himself, that what prayers and struggles we offer to Him in the secret places of our minds and hearts may in fact be more worthy for the very fact that they are seen by Him alone.

There will come a day and there will be a place in which all the secrets of the world will be revealed and the great battles of good and evil each one of us has had to face will be known and revered for what they truly are. In every sincere act of love toward our own best self, toward our family and friends, toward the world at large and most of all toward the One who is our all, we make the transformation from servant to family member happen. We come into union with the God who made us.

May these simple reflections of an extraordinary story give you time to pause and ponder the purpose of your existence and the greatness of the adventure we all experience in this journey called life. We may not bear the ring of power, but in the depth of each of us we carry a soul that is called to live forever with the hidden Lord. It is He who carries us to the mountain top and asks us on a daily basis to practice the virtues which give us the strength to bear the rings of power which haunt our Earthly lives. It is He who humbled Himself even to being born as one of us. It is He who set us the perfect example of all the virtues, most especially of love in which He offered Himself on a cross to pay for our sins.

It was Sam who through his wisdom understood the purpose and value of his existence as portrayed in its deepest mystery through a good story.

" *'Yes, that's so,' said Sam. 'And we shouldn't be here at all if we'd known more about it before we started. But I suppose it's often that way. The brave things in the old tales and songs, Mr. Frodo: adventures, as I used to call them. I used to think*

that they were things the wonderful folk of the stories went out and looked for, because they wanted them, because they were exciting and life was a bit dull, a kind of sport, as you might say. But that's not the way of it with the tales that really mattered, or the ones that stay in the mind. Folk seem to have been just landed in them – usually their paths were laid out that way, as you put it. But I expect they had lots of chances, like us, of turning back, only they didn't. And if they had, we shouldn't know, because they'd be forgotten. We hear about those as just went on – and not all to a good end, mind you; at least not to what folk inside a story and not outside it call a good end. You know, coming home, and finding things all right, though not quite the same – like old Mr. Bilbo. But those aren't always the best tales to hear, though they may be the best tales to get landed in! I wonder what sort of tale we've fallen into?'"
(The Two Towers)

In the end, it was Frodo's mercy which allowed Golum to live and in that virtue he saved himself from himself. Sam's faithfulness and abiding love carried the weight of the struggle and yet brought forth the new life which would carry on the journey of the Hobbit race. In *The Lord of the Rings* there was only one ring of power, whereas we struggle in a world that is inundated with trials and tribulations leading to great variety of evils. But in this world, the power that guides us may be hidden but He has a name, a name above every other name. And we have our own fellowships, broken or not. Through the goodness of the One we are blessed with the very same gifts that Frodo, Sam, Gandalf, Aragorn and all the rest carried; the gifts of virtues and the fruits of the Holy Spirit. May we look at these gifts and fruits and see in them the antidote to the evil temptations which beset us. May we drive back the dark things, which want to come into our world and make it a place of dread. May we be strong enough to throw the evil rings away and bring forth the fruit of new life.

Chapter One
What Makes Our Heroes So Heroic?

FAITH

"Then the prophecies of the old songs have turned out to be true, after a fashion!" said Bilbo.

"Of course!" said Gandalf. "And why should not they prove true? Surely you don't disbelieve the prophecies, because you had a hand in bringing them about yourself? You don't really suppose, do you, that all your adventures and escapes were managed by mere luck, just for your sole benefit? You are a very fine person, Mr. Baggins, and I am very fond of you; but you are only quite a little fellow in a wide world after all." (The Hobbit)

There are three main virtues which we all have heard of even though we may not think of them as such: Faith, Hope and Charity. These virtues have been long called "theological" meaning that they pertain to God. We know what faith is and how useful hope can be and the goodness of charity. But what do these familiar words do for us exactly? How did they play a part in the development of the characters in *The Lord of the Rings*? The truth is that they were indispensable.

Let's begin with Bilbo as he enters the first story and is the engine behind the thrust of the greater story. Faith is defined in *Merriam Webster's Collegiate Dictionary* as "allegiance to duty or person; belief, trust and loyalty to God; something believed with strong conviction." Faith in *The Lord of the Rings* is an act where by the characters are called to believe something they cannot fully explain and cannot even fully understand. That belief leads them to take action and that action demands a commitment. As Bilbo said, "It is a dangerous thing, stepping outside your door….." For the truth of the matter is that any time we take a risk in acting on an inner light, we are depending on a basic underlying faith to guide us. The problem, of course, is to discern who or what is guiding us.

Bilbo ended up taking a journey that led him far from home and all that was familiar but as he struggled against goblins, trolls and a cunning dragon so he relied on something to guide and help him. One might say that he trusted in his basic survival instincts, but I would suggest that in fact he let himself be guided by something he had never known so deeply before. He had within himself a relationship with the greatest force of existence, the force that called him into being and it was this force that helped him in the darkness of Gollum's cave. He did not realize the power contained in the ring he had found but he believed that it fell into his hands for a reason. He believed that he was meant to have it and that despite all the worries and trials he would somehow survive to carry the ring home. He had no sure knowledge of anything but even the reader shared his faith that everything would somehow turn out all right and that the ring does somehow belong to his destiny. It is in the context of this faith that the story becomes believable. And it is in the context of our own lives that we are led to meet the challenges that face us.

Now for us, as for Bilbo, the question becomes "Who is guiding us?" when we cannot see a face or form or even ask the identity of the inner voice. Bilbo did not need to speculate about his Creator; Tolkien took care of all such issues. For us the matter is a little trickier. When we speak to God, we trust He is listening to us. He may respond in a variety of ways, and it is our job to hear Him clearly. For many this involves nothing more than listening to a whisper inside the head or heart. For others there are little tests that they put up to God, for example, "I will open the Bible randomly and on the page I come to I will find my answer." Some see in the events in their lives the acts of God leading them in a certain direction: for example, there is a parking space miraculously open in front of the store, so God must want me to go in and buy something. God surely does try to reach us in a myriad of ways, but often we bumble about quite certain that God has spoken when there is the possibility that God is simply allowing the world to work as it naturally does, and He is waiting for us to settle down and pay attention to Him rather than to our little games.

There is only one way to know if God is speaking to us and that is the way that Jesus Christ told us, "By the fruit will the tree be known." The only problem is that we have to take some action and yet wait for fruit and sometimes the fruit doesn't even ripen in our lifetimes. So what comfort do we have then? As you notice in Bilbo's and Frodo's adventure, they both felt reluctant to take the lead in the adventures that were waiting for them. Their experiences harkened more to Jesus' command to "pick up your cross and follow me." Both Bilbo and Frodo were cast into settings where they were asked to do things that they had not looked for. They found themselves being transformed by roles that forced them to do things that they had never imagined. If you study the lives of the saints you find the same pattern. None of the apostles quite got what he bargained for. Saint Paul definitely found himself in a role he would never have imagined.

So how do we live a life of faith as did Bilbo and Frodo? How do we respond to the whisper of God in our lives? For one, expect that when God is speaking He will not offer a life of ease and plenty. He never offered that while on Earth and He does not suggest such to His listeners in the gospels. He is God and He can offer us a wide variety of ways of picking up our crosses and following Him. But do not imagine that we have the whole picture even when we think we know exactly what He wants. The Lord tends to be surprising. So, we are left with faith in an unseen God, a hidden figure that guides us and loves us but often asks us to do hard things. But is He entirely hidden? No, thank goodness. He left us His word and His church. If we believe in God at all, we are led to the knowledge of His perfection and goodness. Would a perfect God leave us alone to fend for ourselves in a world with so many distractions, temptations and outright evils? It would simply not make sense. Thus the God who gave us His son did not leave us but guides us still.

Bilbo and Frodo had to rely on a guide. They both had Gandalf near at hand. Who was Gandalf? He was a wizard who lived in the time of "long ago." Now, in Tolkien's time I often wonder if there was as much controversy about witches and wizards as there is today. To him, perhaps, a wizard was someone who was deep in the knowledge of the mysterious and hidden world of the spirit. He was one who studied and knew such things and was capable of understanding and respecting the power of such a realm. Whom does Gandalf represent to us? Let us look at whom the Lord Jesus said He would leave as a guide for all of time. He said to Peter, "You are my rock and upon this rock I will build my church." His words were clear. He had built the foundation of a church, and He expected the leaders of that church to follow the example He set the night of the Last Supper. As He washed the feet of His disciples, so He told them to imitate His example to be the servants of all. We are all called to serve God, but ministers, deacons, priests, bishops and popes are in fact the servants of us all in that they are called to be our guides as well as leaders. As a matter of fact, a person who is being considered for the cause of sainthood is referred to as "the servant of God".

So, was Gandalf a priestly figure dressed in the garb of a wizard? It is possible that Tolkien never thought of such a thing. But it is certain that he was a guide who counseled and led in a spirit of love and service. Thus faith is not completely blind. Bilbo and Frodo were not alone. They had help and so do we. They were given the history of their people and the songs that told the stories of people from all realms and all generations. We have the Bible and the gifts of Traditions, which embody the lives of the faithful who have walked before us. The words of God are faithfully recorded so as to give us insight as to the will of God from the beginning of time. And He left us his faithful servants in the magisterium of the church; those who can help us to discern His voice and comfort us in the carrying of a particularly painful cross. Faith in God rules us while faith in His Word and His church guide us.

There were times when Gandalf was absent or unable to perform his function as guide, and both Bilbo and Frodo were required to walk in darkness. And so it happens with us at times. Mortal men are human and there are those who are not faithful to their calling and position. Sin is a part of our broken nature. At such times we are forced to look for a new guide who is faithful and often that will be someone who, like Gandalf, found his position as guide a burden as well as a delight. If a guide loses his faith and does not accept the cross, preach the cross, and live the cross, then he cannot truly call himself one of the faithful, much less a guide. The darkness we experience may be a time of purification so as better to see the light of God's mysterious grace when the physical guidance of a leader is absent.

Faith is a word that awakens a lot of emotions in all of us. It is the cornerstone of all virtues for without faith there can be no love. You must believe that that which you love exists in order to love it. And Hope springs forth from faith in that you must believe in the light of God, even in the darkness of evil, in order to give hope a chance to breathe. As Mother Teresa of Calcutta said on several occasions, "We are not called to be successful but rather to be faithful." We are all called to be men and women of Faith. Thank God.

Hope

"There is naught that you can do, other than to resist, with hope or without it. But you do not stand alone..."

"That is the purpose for which you are called hither. Called, I say, though I have not called you to me, strangers from distant lands. You have come and are here met, in this very nick of time, by chance as it may seem. Yet it is not so. Believe rather that it is so ordered that we, who sit here, and none others, must now find counsel for the peril of the world." (The Fellowship of the Ring)

Hope is defined in *Merriam Webster's Collegiate Dictionary* as "a desire accompanied by expectation of or belief in fulfillment." For a long time I thought of Sam as simply the most faith filled character in the whole book and thus I considered him my favorite character. It takes a lot to remain faithful even when the sun's light seems dim and there is little beauty anywhere. Yet, in my recent rereading of the story I was struck more so by the fact that Sam, as an example par excellence, believed that things would turn out for the best, even when he admitted he had no hope. It is a strange position to take to be sure, but there are times when we must admit that we do not have any reasonable cause to hope a situation will improve yet we simply refuse to give up. Sam went beyond that point. He went so far as to admit that he didn't even have the heart to hope, and he was too exhausted and worn out to carry the burden of hope, yet almost against his own will, he kept trying to finish the job and believed that he was going to accomplish what he set out to do even if his hopes had to be adjusted to the dismal possibility that he would never live to see the fruit of his efforts. That is steadfast hope.

As Christians, we are called upon to live out that kind of faithful witness to the God who is hope itself. God's mind may not correspond to our mind, and God's thoughts may not be the same as our thoughts. What we base our hope on will not always add up in the accounting machine of worldly reality. Miracles happen. Sometimes the miracle may be something that only we know about. A man may never tell anyone about the incident when he fell asleep at the wheel and woke to see the semi coming head on but in that instant of prayer somehow the car did what cars do not normally do, and he lived on to ponder the incident many a time since then. Many people I know have had at least one experience in which they were astonished by something happening, which comforted them at a death or helped them in life. The tragic thing is that there are many who would scoff at such things as if to say that God would never bother with such trivial incidents or with such personal moments. How strange and sad to dismiss God's intimate role in our daily lives. Yes, the car could have swerved and done a two wheelie, perhaps it is within the range of mechanical possibilities, but how does that alter the reality that God was present at that moment, and He played His part in assisting us? To ignore the eternal care of the One who created us is dangerous in that it tends to limit our thinking so that we put God in a box and insist that "He wouldn't bother to do that."

Hope is based on our faith that every day, in everything we do, God is with us and that everything does matter, even those things no one else knows about. Perhaps more so when God is our only witness. Remember the incidence of the Elvish rope that Sam needed and how after it had helped them get down a difficult cliff he wanted it back and it fell quietly at his feet though it had been tied securely high out of reach? He was given a glimpse of a hidden hand that cared for him. So we can see in the course of our ordinary days many such glimpses of Divine Providence.

Did the sun come up today? Did you hope for it? Probably not in your conscious mind but on some level you had hope and faith that the sun would continue to exist and that the Earth would stay on its present course and so you expected to see the sun. Granted, it may have been quite overcast but the sun was still there. Even more, there might have been a dreadful storm and a tornado may have hit your neighborhood but still the sun rose. Many people passed on through the night to the other side but for those of us left here to work out our salvation, the sun is with us. There is a miracle. There is an ordinary miracle that most of us forget to praise God for. In fact, the sun is rising and setting somewhere in the world at every minute of the day. Yet the Good Lord does not get exhausted with making gorgeous sunsets and sunrises every single day. More amazing still, He has been making sunrises and sunsets every single minute of every day since the world began. There is faithful providence that we can have great hope in.

Another aspect of the virtue of hope that Sam demonstrates is the fact that he hoped to finish a task that was not even properly his. The one who carried the burden of evil was weak and had no strength to go on. It was then up to Sam, the character with undying hope, to carry not only the ring bearer but also the ring. And he found the burden light. This depiction in the book is so thought-provoking that this experience of Sam played itself over in my mind for many days. I tried to think how do we carry "ring bearers"? At first I could only think of how we carry our own sin in our own lives, but then it hit me, we carry each other's sins many times. How many people have loved an alcoholic? Or a drug addict? Or someone who is suffering from great depression? There are so many ways that those we love may be burdened by personal sin or the sins inflicted on them by others. And what is our response? "I don't want to deal with this? He doesn't deserve a good woman like me? I don't have time for such trouble?"

It is a very good thing that our Lord is more like Sam than us. It is a very good thing that there are Sams out there who will not give up hope. Take a saint, pretty much any saint, and you will find a person who worked with the poor, the sick, the hopeless, the tragic, and the dirty and troubled people on this Earth. Poor in spirit can apply to those who have no hope and who feel they cannot carry the burden of their lives any more. It is then that we must look at ourselves and ask, do I help the hopeless? Do I help to carry the burden of others?

It is not too hard to give money, at least some money. But it is very hard to carry another's burden. It was a pretty intimate thing Sam did. Notice the many times he took care of Frodo's needs. He fetched water and shared his food. He refused sleep and watched over the form of his exhausted friend. He caressed his hand and forehead. He loved Frodo in a very personal way. He encouraged him and helped him, and he simply would not allow Frodo to give up. And when Frodo did break down, he picked him up and carried him. Do we do that with our brothers and sisters much less with employers and neighbors?

What was our Lord thinking when He asked us to carry one another's burdens and do unto others as we would have them do for us? Forgive our enemies? Love those who hate us? These are crazy words which do not fit well with a world that demands a right to happiness and freedom from pain. Yet, it is in this very commitment to serving and carrying each other's burdens that the hope of all rests. It is no small comparison that Tolkien makes when he has Sam carry the burden of his hopeless friend on whom all hopes are based. "…your quest stands upon the edge of a knife. Stray but a little and it will fail, to the ruin of all. Yet hope remains while all the company is true."

We stray all the time, but God forgives us and we are allowed to live one more day to try to right the wrongs which face us. And there are those among us who do remain true through all sorts of evil circumstances. Their faithfulness rebuilds our faith not only in ourselves and mankind in general but also in the reality of hope itself.

Hope is a virtue which causes us great joy, and when it is absent we may as well wish to be dead. But for the hope that is beyond all hope, we would have perished as a race long ago. Those who sacrificed themselves in wars so that evil would not conquer, those who refused to recant their faith and suffered terrible martyrdoms teach us the value and purpose of hope. Those who live quiet lives of suffering physically or emotionally express the greatness of the virtue of hope. We would cease to be who we are without hope, and the world just might not continue to revolve around the sun without hope. Our hope is based on our faith in the One who transcended even death. Even when we are blinded by tears and our hearts are breaking by the sorrows that we all must suffer, we cannot give up hope. It is this transcending virtue which calls us home and gives new life to a failing spirit.

Charity

"Then as he had kept watch Sam had noticed that at times a light seemed to be shining faintly within; but now the light was even clearer and stronger. Frodo's face was peaceful, the marks of fear and care had left it; but it looked old, old and beautiful, as if the chiseling of the shaping years was now revealed in many fine lines that had before been hidden, though the identity of the face was not changed. Not that Sam Gamgee put it that way to himself. He shook his head, as if finding words useless, and murmured: 'I love him. He's like that, and sometimes it shines through, somehow. But I love him, whether or no.'" (The Two Towers)

Charity is defined in *Merriam Webster's Collegiate Dictionary* as "benevolent good will or love of humanity." I would have to say that the whole Fellowship was a lesson in charity. There are so many ways in which the various characters bring out the truth of each theological virtue that it is really a matter of personal taste to pick a certain character for a certain virtue. This is by no means an exhaustive list of the possibilities, but rather here are some thoughts that may fuel more thoughts, which in the end may lead to convictions which are the basis of all noble actions.

As I say, I could pick several characters who display charity for there is much of that virtue in *The Lord of the Rings* but because he was such an intriguing character I will focus on Faramir. Here was a man not well loved by his own father who was given the chance of a lifetime. It is something to reject the power and glory of an evil temptation but how many of us have faced the possibility of winning a loved one's respect or "love" if we but do a possibly evil deed? Faramir was a man with a noble heart. His love was that of one who was not looking for something in exchange, not even reciprocal love.

Love can be divided into three categories. There is physical love on the level of sexual desire. It can refer to love of the body and meeting its basic needs as well as desire for the physical love of another. Next, there is the love of family and friends, basically a relationship based love in which you usually reciprocate with members of your intimate circle. Finally, there is a spiritual love also referred to in the sense of "brotherhood of mankind." In this last spirit-based love you do not need to be loved in return. In fact, it is the very nature of this love to be so completely unselfish that no reciprocation is even desired. One loves simply for Love's sake. How does Faramir fit in? When Faramir meets Frodo and Sam as they are being led into Mordor by Gollum, it is Faramir who is out fighting and protecting his people and finds the Hobbits and takes them under his wing. If you only saw the movie and did not read the book, you might want to take a look at this portion of the book for Faramir is quite differently depicted in the two versions. In the book, he does not desire the ring. He did not even allow himself to be tempted by the power it represented though it could have done him much good in the eyes of his father. His father dearly wanted to have the ring for himself, and when Boromir failed in that task Faramir was not even considered a suitable replacement for the father was obsessed with the first son. But had Faramir held the ring of power before Denethor's grasp there might have been a change of fortunes. Faramir might have become the favored son even if only in memory. The fact that the ring would have corrupted Denethor as it corrupted all who held onto it was not lost on Faramir. Even while he was still trying to figure out the riddle of what the "bane" was, he told Frodo that he wanted no part of it. When its mystery was unlocked for him he took no steps to grasp what was not his and what he realized would only bring harm to the people of his world. He was wise as well as good. He really wished for the good of all mankind as well as Hobbit kind and all the rest that lived in Middle-earth.

To love is a very intimate thing, but when one's love is centered on a personal need then it loses some of its good. For example, if a mother loves her son so much that she gives him everything that he wants, she does him actual harm. To give someone everything they want is to fear their disapproval and to want to be loved in return more than to care about the welfare of the other. To fear injury or separation to such a degree that a child cannot grow is to satisfy one's own craving for security rather than to truly love.

When Faramir attempts to fulfill the demands of his father by attempting to retake a lost outpost, he is showing a complete selflessness to the fate which awaits him. When he is being healed and meets Eowyn, he knows she is in love with Aragorn, yet he is not insulted that she has loved another or that Aragorn is a greater man in the kingdom. He sees the truth of Eowyn; that she wants what she cannot have, but he loves her with an acceptance of her faults even before she can see him for who he is in his own right. Faramir plays a fairly small part in the whole book, but he is such an outstanding example of the highest form of love that he needs to be highlighted. As Faramir loves, sacrifices, and accepts the faults of his friends and family so Christ does the same for us. Faramir is not God but he does a mighty good job following the example of perfect love that our Father presented for us in the form of His son.

How do we witness this love in our own lives? What does the good Lord ask of us when He says, "Follow me."? Perhaps it is not terribly complicated but is awfully hard to accept. To love all of humankind as a brother and sister is to always be attentive to the needs of others. In the United States it is a fact that Americans use a grossly disproportionate amount of the world's resources. We eat better, live in bigger, nicer homes and have more security than most of the world. Would it be good for us to be destitute? No. Poverty does not ensure a spirit of love. Though I must say; that many saints and simply saintly people have given up secure lifestyles to live "as one with the poor." But the Lord never said, "Be poor." He did say that it was harder for a rich man to enter the kingdom than for a camel to pass through the eye of the needle.

So how do we "love" our brother? Well, the answer is so familiar that you can read on with your eyes shut. "As you do it for the least of my brothers so you do it for me... Feed the hungry, give water to the thirsty, visit the sick, visit the imprisoned, shelter the homeless..." Granted, you may not be in any position to join the Peace Corps or work as a missionary, but there are nursing homes with elderly who could use some attention and probably there are some homes for children where help would be appreciated. Foster care, mentoring, bringing food and comfort to the elderly, bringing the word of God to prisoners, teaching in after school programs, offering up vacation money to help a village in Guatemala buy a pig... There are as many ways to serve our brothers and sisters as there are ways to love.

The amazing thing is that when one loves, all humanity it seems that one can in fact love one's family better than ever before. And strangely enough the family might learn a thing or two about happiness as well. Once we realize that every person is loved by God so much that He would sacrifice himself to save any one of us, we gain a new perspective. Love ceases to be about our need to be filled, our desire to be liked, our wish to be well thought of and it becomes not only more awesome but a bit more sensible too. My pastor was asked how much was a person supposed to give to church and he said, "If it doesn't hurt a bit then it isn't sacrificial love, and we are called to a sacrificial love." We are called to love our husbands and wives when they are far from perfect and even when they are broken with sin. We are called to love our children when they have worn us out and we are so tired we can't think anymore. We are called to love our brothers and sisters when they have taken different paths and seem little less than strangers. We are called to love the stranger in the store, to smile and be helpful even when someone slips ahead of us in line. We are called to love the ragged, homeless person who litters the corners and makes our cities less pleasant places. Love does not always demand money or even a personal intervention. Sometimes we are not able to intervene; it is simply not possible, as in the case of a war on the other side of the world. But prayers are real expressions of love, and they do matter. Deep, sincere prayer led the saints towards the gates of Heaven.

There is also the aspect of simply being less self-absorbed. This may seem obvious but there can be a lot of issues behind it. Remember Tom Bombadil? He was a very cheerful fellow who came to the aid of Frodo and companions early in their adventures. If it were not for his power to keep order in his forest and hold the evil forces at bay, surely the simple Hobbits would never have accomplished their mission. He was a man who wanted no trouble from the world at large, yet he accommodated the needs of weary, unknown travelers who had lost their way. He not only took good care of his little patch of the planet, but he cared for those who came into his world.

The issue of stewardship can come in here in that we are stewards of the Earth. When we think of our needs first we are often led to think that there is nothing wrong with getting the most we can get at the cheapest price. But our brothers and sisters are affected by what we do even if we do not care to look deeply into the issue. Where do our clothes, food, tools and toys come from? Are the people who make them being paid a fair wage or are they virtual slaves to feed a monstrous economy which has no soul? Can we repair anything that we have bought or will it be added to the multi-story, skyscraper, junk heap that is put in someone else's back yard? What has happened to all the small family farms and businesses? Did actual sacrificial love play a part in their demise or was it simply that everyone found it profitable and easier to go to the big shopping centers which have virtually taken over every town and city? Does it matter that I waste? Does it hurt anyone that I have way more than I need? Is it wrong in the eyes of God that I run an air conditioner when I get the least bit warm, and I hate to be uncomfortable to the point where I will pay to have all my creature comforts met at all times? If Faramir had been thinking about his needs, he would never have been the man he was. The same can be said for Aragorn, Gandalf, Frodo, Sam and a multitude of other characters. Taking care of ourselves with little thought to the larger context of our actions as a way of life is not terribly noble, and it hardly reflects the love that God has for us.

So, how do we take the lessons that Faramir offers us? First we do not try to gain for ourselves power, glory and a life of comfort. These are dangerous temptations even when veiled in the desire to gain the approval or love of someone dear to us. And when an opportunity comes to do good, we do it. In fact we seek out opportunities to do good, and we try very hard to not let the left hand know what the right hand is doing. What Our Father sees in secret will be rewarded justly. We must love with our eyes open to the truth of those around us. We know that no one is perfect, and we love them anyway. We know that most people have a broken, chipped part to themselves and sometimes there are terrible cracks of sin coursing through the whole of God's created work, but we love them anyway. The more imperfect the object of our love, the more clearly we see them and give them what they most truly need: friendship, work, money, food, a good joke, a shove in the right direction, and thus the greater the love.

Where have we come in our travels with the three theological virtues? Faith leads us to see God even though He may be hidden. We believe that we were created for a reason, that we have value and are loved by the Creator. Hope springs from our faith, and we find ourselves capable of hoping even when there is little or nothing to support our hope. What do we hope for? We hope that good is stronger than evil, that there is life after death and that God is just. For hope to lead us, we must accept that the fruit of our diligence may not be apparent until the time is ripe and that may be well beyond our human expectations. Hope just continues to hope as need be. Charity is the culmination of our faith and hope. Love is in some sense the creative expression of faith and hope. If we do not act on our faith and hope, can we truly say we know God? He is an ever vigilant creative being, and to be perfect as He calls us to be demands many daily acts of selfless love. We pray to and converse with our God who asks much of us but offers more than we can possibly imagine. He offers us a transformation into children of God who will live forever and ever with Him on an Earth remade in His perfection. We will be going home.

That may be why the Shire holds such attraction for many of us. We all know that craving, to go to the home where all living things are nurtured, everything is beautiful and all is well with those who live there. Who wants to live on clouds? No, we crave a home that is built of the good Earth and where all things reflect the goodness of God. Faith, hope and charity can take us far. The road is hard and we may meet a few orcs and cave trolls along the way, but do not fear, we are not alone; the cardinal virtues will help us find our way.

Chapter Two
Warriors Awake!

"He cast aside his cloak and a white light shone forth like a sword in that black place. Before his upraised hand the foul Messenger recoiled, and Gandalf coming seized and took from him the tokens: coat, cloak, and sword. 'These we will take in memory of our friend,' he cried. 'But for your terms, we reject them utterly. Get you gone, for your embassy is over and death is near to you. We did not come here to waste words in treating with Sauron, faithless and accursed; still less with one of his slaves. Begone!'" (The Return of the King)

There are four cardinal virtues and they are: prudence, justice, fortitude and temperance. I propose to add a little twist in this chapter in that I want to look not only at the characters who demonstrated these virtues but take a close look at those characters who defied these virtues. This can mean a difference as great as heaven or hell. It is rather startling how a misunderstanding of one of these virtues can corrupt our path and lead us into very dark places.

Prudence

" *'Leave it to the Ents!' said Treebeard. 'We shall search the valley from head to foot and peer under every pebble. Trees are coming back to live here, old trees, wild trees. The Watchwood we will call it. Not a squirrel will go here, but I shall know of it. Leave it to the Ents! Until seven times the years in which he tormented us have passed, we shall not tire of watching him.'"*
(The Two Towers)

Prudence is defined as the ability to govern and discipline oneself by the use of reason. In the character of Legolas, I saw a great deal that reminded me of angels. In *The Simarillion*, Tolkien creates a time before time when the world was just being formed and elves were among the first folk created. Granted, those who have read *The Simarillion* know there is a whole lot more to that story but to keep our thoughts in focus it helps to take one point at a time. Elves were among the first folk and they were created to live forever as higher life forms that were close not only to the song of creation but to the thought that was creation itself. In other words, they knew a lot about life on Earth and the world beyond. Legolas was not afraid of the dead because he knew he was not going to die so death had no power to threaten him. There is a case to be made that the elves were in fact angel-types.

Now, before we move on we have to come to some decision. Do we believe in angels? If you are a follower of Jesus Christ you know that He affirms the existence of angels in a myriad of situations. For example He tells the apostles, {Matt. Xviii 10} "See that you despise not one of these little ones; for I say to you, that their angels in heaven always see the face of my Father who is in heaven." He was also ministered to by angels after the trial of forty days in the desert. The Old Testament speaks of angels so many times it would take quite a while to list all the references, but a couple examples are when Abraham serves the angels of God who have come to see him, when Jacob wrestles with an angel, and when Tobias is led on a journey by a faithful angel. In the teachings of the Catholic Church, angels are part of the Tradition of faith. Every person is given a guardian angel to look after the welfare of that particular soul. Once again we are met with an aspect of our existence on Earth that is shrouded in mystery. We may believe in angels but we don't know everything there is to know about them. What we do know is rather basic. Everyone has one, maybe more, and they are usually hidden and their purpose is to serve so as to help a soul gain eternal salvation. There are those who have seen their guardian angels and there are times in life when most of us, realizing it or not, have had invaluable assistance that we cannot explain but which could well have come from our guardian angel.

Let us look at Legolas and the virtue of prudence. Legolas was definitely a friend who sought to serve those who needed him. He had extraordinary abilities. He could see far, and he could see the spirits of the dead. He was very intelligent, and he did not seem as weighed down by the needs of most people. Perhaps the most important talent that Legolas displayed was his prudence. He was not one to jump into things without thought. He saw the worth of his friends but he was not blind to their faults. He was willing to disagree when necessary and even argue a point though he always bowed to the higher authority. His had a nature firmly committed to the truth though he was willing to accept that he was not infallible. He was not God, and he knew it. He accepted his place. He was wise but never belligerent. Everything about Legolas spoke of a character who was content to be who he was but yet strove to be the very best he could be. Prudence is defined in *Merriam Webster's Collegiate Dictionary* as "the ability to govern and discipline oneself by the use of reason, shrewdness in the management of affairs, skill in the use of resources and caution." Legolas was all this and more. He was not simply prudent; he was prudence with a heart. Perhaps it was this last quality that took the edge off what we usually think of when we imagine a prudent person. But in any case, he was the very flower of prudence.

Now, let us look at someone who was not so prudent. Who was someone who lacked self-discipline at times, was hardly known for being shrewd, and at times seemed to court danger? How about Pippin? It was Pippin who accidentally awoke the Balrog in the mines of Moria by an incautious act. It was Pippin who looked into the palantir through a lack of self-control. It was Pippin who spoke out of turn and offered his service to Denenthor even as that Steward was going mad. Now, to Pippin's credit, he had a large heart, and a lot of the mischief he caused was offset by the greatness of his charity to others and the world at large. But just the same, let us take a look at what prudence and its lack can mean to us. The case could be made that Denenthor was a man who let the virtue of prudence get twisted into an outright evil. Denenthor knew more than was good for him and though he may have once been a good leader he lost that ability when he conformed himself to the information he had learned from the palantir at the will of the great eye. He was willing to do what no man in his right mind would be able to force himself to do, namely kill himself and his son. He was being cautious to an extreme when he decided that it was better to burn now and get it over with rather than wait for the enemy to come upon him. Denenthor was a case where "prudence" is no longer prudence except in name only. He thought he was wise and controlled, but he had slipped into madness. So what then if Pippin's lack of prudence is not so bad and Denenthor's overabundance of worldly prudence was the gateway to despair? The difference was in the two other virtues of humility and charity. Pippin was humble in his own silly way, and he carried within himself a deep and abiding love for those he cherished. Denethor may have loved his sons, but his love was one with strings attached. His pride ruled all. Prudence is an excellent virtue, but few of us have the supernatural skills of Legolas to witness this virtue so perfectly. When we err, it is good to remember that humility and charity do much to offset our lack of discipline, shrewdness and skill to handle all events that come our way.

How do we try to perfect the bit of prudence we might have? Again, this is not something that is considered of great value in a world where freedom of speech is at times interpreted to mean, "Say whatever you want," and even, "Show whatever you want, and do whatever you want." Too often we are given the image of a "prude" when thinking of prudence, but really nothing could be further from the truth for to be prudent involves interaction with others in an effective manner by being self-disciplined, exercising skills, and being cautious. The old adage, "Think before you speak." would apply here. And so would "Think before you act." It has been said that it was a custom among certain Native Americans to consider the consequence of an action down to the seventh generation. Granted, that is beyond most of us but there is food for thought. Prudence involves deep pondering. To gain skills, knowledge and self-discipline one must be alone with one's thoughts or learning just won't take place. If the T.V. is always on, or the radio constantly blaring or we are forever running the kids around to sport programs and craft classes, do we ever get any chance to think about anything seriously? How about our kids? If we are the typical two-working-parent house and the laundry has to get done sometime this week, and it would be nice to see the spouse if not actually talk to him about something other than scheduling, then the question arises, are we being prudent? Or rather are we running as if the very whips of Sauron are at our backs? What is life about? Does it have meaning? Am I called to do something by God that I am refusing to act on? Do I even acknowledge that I have an immortal soul and I will live forever, SOMEWHERE? Do I care where? Prudence is a virtue because our lives do matter and because God has called each one of us into being for a reason. It is the height of prudence to care to make time and space so as to heed His voice.

JUSTICE

" ... 'likely enough that we are going to our doom: the last march of the Ents. But if we stayed at home and did nothing, doom would find us anyway, sooner or later. That thought has long been growing in our hearts; and that is why we are marching now. It was not a hasty resolve. Now at least the last march of the Ents may be worth a song. Aye,' he sighed, 'we may help the other peoples before we pass away.'" (The Two Towers)

Justice, as defined by *Merriam-Webster's Collegiate Dictionary* is simple. "Conformity to truth, fact, or reason." Treebeard is an excellent character for many reasons, but the one I find most compelling is that he is a being of justice. He was not emotionally invested with the overwhelming desire for revenge though we can imagine that he felt some bit of pleasure in taking apart the evil compound of destruction that Saruman had created for himself. But being a thoughtful character, he was not driven by the hasty emotional elements that most of us are. When he took action, it was the culmination of long thought and it was based on the overwhelming evidence that a grave injustice was being done. He needed to take part in the correction of an ongoing tragedy. Treebeard did his job, and he did it thoroughly. He did not seek out his enemy to destroy him but rather he sought to simply end his ability to do harm. In the end he let Saruman go free, not because Saruman had shown signs of conversion, but simply because he saw his work well and justly completed. Treebeard was a character you could trust because his justice extended to all things. He was not only obliging to Merry and Pippin {once he knew they were not orcs}, but his charity also extended itself as much as possible to helping anyone in need and seeing to their comfort.

Justice alone would be a very frightening virtue, for if we gave everyone exactly what they deserved, this poor world would soon be overwhelmed. I suspect that is why babies are so cute and little children have to be excused for their faults so often: because we must experience a great deal of mercy before we ever grow into adulthood, so we can learn to offer it to each other. Pippin and Merry were but babes in the woods to Treebeard. He was the wise councilor and friend. Though they knew much more about the current events of Middle-earth, Treebeard knew the eternal things. He knew that justice must be balanced by mercy. Letting Saruman go was more than an act of justice because the case could have been made that Saruman deserved death for his crimes—but yet he was allowed to live. He was even allowed to go free. Mercy always leaves open the possibility of betrayal. But it also allows for the possibility of redemption and makes the virtues of justice stronger and more potent.

Who was a character who lacked the true spirit if justice? There are several possibilities; but the one who stands out, beyond the Eye which was blind to justice, and Saruman who was corrupted and could not see truth much less justice, was Gollum. The earliest historical fact we know about Gollum is that he killed his cousin to get the ring, claiming it as a birthday present. From then on Gollum's whole existence is marred by a lack of justice. Everything is misunderstood and wrongly accused in his twisted mind. Even the very light of the sun becomes a source of punishment to him. He torments himself by going against his own healthy nature and takes to living in dark, damp places, tearing away at raw, unclean fish or whatever else would be available, and we suspect repugnant to a normal person. The ring torments him by giving him an unnaturally long life and abilities beyond his natural sphere. Yet it lets go of him despite his unswerving devotion to it and attaches itself to Bilbo. Gollum never blames the ring but rather Bilbo and then Frodo. He is forever seeing himself as the victim while he clings to his very victim status.

The role of victim is a very common one in our society today. If we are not allowed to get what we want when we want or if we suffer in the least bit, even if it is the natural outcome of our own actions—for example, smoking or eating too much or eating the wrong kind of food or living in a hectic environment or spoiling our kids—we tend to see, in a tormented sort of way, that we are not being cared for and life is not fair. The fact that we are not properly caring for ourselves, our things, our families or our society, rarely comes into our conscious thought. There are very few who want to take responsibility, much less the blame, for our personal or social ills.

As with Gollum, his lack of justice in his early life leads to a warping of the whole course of his life. He continues, despite options to reform, to fall back on the Gollum personality which drives his sick mind.

He misunderstands Sam, who calls him a "sneak," and clings to that epithet to reinforce an old grudge; thus he never comes to peace within or without. Gollum wants to be angry with the world. He has a vested interest in blaming Sam for being a fat, nasty Hobbit who cares nothing for the inner struggle inside of Smeagol. Sam, it is true, does not much care for Smeagol, but in truth it is not his place to heal his wounds and make everything better inside by loving him despite all the evil that Gollum had done and was still capable of planning. Sam simply was not able to give Smeagol what he wanted, and thus once again when faced with an unkind remark or a demand, Smeagol chose to take the victim role rather than see the injustice of his own evaluations. Sam could have been nicer, but it would hardly have fitted the role of protector to Frodo. Even if Sam had been gentler with Gollum, one wonders if it would have made any difference. The ring had claimed Gollum from head to toe so long he was a mere shadow of his former self. Since justice was completely absent from the mind and soul of Gollum, there was little to lead us to believe that he would have been converted by just a bit more kindness on Sam's part or on anyone else's part.

It is sad that Smeagol is not a redeemed character and that his death is as pitiful as his life in his being swallowed up by the fires of Mount Doom. It is not because others failed to give him what he needed as much as that he chose self-interest over justice in the first place. Justice is based on a firm grasp of the truth in any given situation. Gollum was a master of self-deception and therefore he not only offered no justice to others, he suffered a supreme lack of justice to his very nature, even to the point of sacrificing his life to a doom of no redemption.

How do we look at justice in our own lives? Is justice something that we demand of others whether we offer it or not? Do we look at the situations in our own lives as if everyone is responsible for what happens to us? Or do we accept the fact that the wife we have, the job we have, the house we have, and even our kids are a product of our own decisions and the grace we have been given or refused from above? If we see ourselves as the most important people in the universe, then we tend to find that nothing matches up to our expectations. We suffer from disappointment on a continual basis. Life is not fair because "we deserve better."

But if we see ourselves as we truly are, as servants of the Most High, then our perspective changes drastically. First of all, we find that life is not meant to be a great joy going from one pleasurable experience to the next: for our Lord told us that we are to pick up our cross and follow him. That does not sound like a lot of fun. Also, He reminds us that the servant cannot be better than the Master, and that if the world treated Him badly our fate would be to suffer likewise. There is not a lot of room for self-pity here. If we see ourselves as workers in the Master's vineyard, then He can help us, guide us, and protect us from evil, but not from suffering. In other words, He never says we will not feel the effects of sin and evil but rather we will avoid becoming evil and suffering the fate of the damned if we follow Him faithfully.

We can now look at life with a different attitude. If we are not dealing with a major crisis or a terrible illness it is easier to be grateful and see things more as a gift rather than, "not good enough." How the world seems to change when we have an attitude of gratitude! And that kind of attitude more nearly fits the reality of who we truly are. We are not God nor are we kings or queens of the universe who deserve by our mere existence to have all things go well. Is it just that we suffer? The case could be made that suffering to some extent is a result of being in the family of God. Because we are connected to each other as fellow human beings, we gain by the goodness of some, and we suffer by the evil of all. We want everyone to get exactly what he or she deserves in this world, and we tend to be disappointed when the selfish and greedy get more than the humble, gentle spirits who deserve good things more. Here we end up back at the dual concepts of faith and hope. If we believe in God and He is just, then we have hope in a place and a time where all things will be fulfilled according to justice. Do we want to be served with strict justice?—For our Lord assured us that as we do unto others so it would be done unto us? Remember mercy! Yes, it would probably be a very good thing to remember mercy so that when our turn to stand before the throne of perfect justice comes, we get to hope for some mercy coming our way.

God Himself has already shown us the mystery of His mercy in His sacrificial love for us. It would behoove us to keep His death on the cross in mind when we hold the fate of someone else in our hands. For, we demand justice on Earth but then we will be asking for mercy at the end of time. None of us, in all honesty, could say that we would long survive perfect justice before the throne of God. We all sin against God in a myriad of ways, and we all at different points tend to put ourselves first and explain away or simply ignore the commands of God. At times it seems as if the world just does not take the Lord very seriously. Since He hasn't punished us as we would those who thwart our will, so we figure He is a relatively benign Old Gentleman who will understand when we get up there to explain things to Him. This can be a rather dangerous position to take: for our Lord promised us that each person would have to pay to the last penny his or her due. His mercy is that He gives us time to work things out here on Earth, and we are given so many miracles, so many good guides, so many holy examples, so many warnings, and so many whispers in the soul, that we can never claim that we simply didn't know what He wanted from us. We just would rather do our own thing. Justice is a wonderful blessing, but it is also a double-edged sword.

As we demand justice so we must also give justice and that means facing the truth of our lives and the responsibility we face in the part we have played to mess it up or waste it or corrupt it. So we pray for conversion, which leads to redemption, so that mercy will live in us, and we will bear the fruit of a life well lived.

FORTITUDE

"Then Merry heard of all sounds in that hour the strangest. It seemed that Dernhelm laughed, and the clear voice was like the ring of steel. 'But no living man am I! You look upon a woman. Eowyn I am, Eomund's daughter. You stand between me and my lord and kin. Begone, if you are not deathless! For living or dark undead, I will smite you, if you touch him.'" (The Return of the King)

Fortitude was a virtue shared by many characters in the Lord of the Rings. It is defined in *Merriam-Webster's Collegiate Dictionary* as "strength of mind that enables a person to encounter danger or bear pain or adversity with courage." The maiden Eowyn comes to mind in a special way. She experienced a supreme moment in which all the little aspects of her character had to be forged together into a solid whole, which could withstand the terrible evil of the Lord of the Nazgul. She had been a woman looking for a fight not so much because she didn't understand the power and worth of her femininity but because she heard to the depth of her being a call to do something great. She confused that something great with the battles that the men went off to fight in the name of all that is good and just. She wanted desperately to be a part of that great struggle and thus show her worth both as a woman and as a person. Her experience of life had formed her in such a way that she felt prepared to do more than the daily hardships of being a good sister, niece, and citizen of her land. She craved a venue in which to express her supernatural desire to be greater than the sum of her parts, to be transformed into something truly great.

It is not an uncommon wish on most people's part to be in some way recognized as great, even if the matter be something as common as a community sport team or to simply have the greatest garden, house, car or artistic talent. Our desire may spring from a false belief that God would not really come to Earth and die for us ordinary folks who never accomplish anything other than the usual job, dishes, laundry, meals, and so forth. We hardly seem able to justify our existence. That God is a mystery who does as He sees fit and that He sees fit to love us even in our most ordinary day and common experiences seems a bit baffling. The supernatural love of God hardly seems possible in the completely natural world we live in. Yet, ironically, that is one of the most touching things about the whole Hobbit adventure story. It is the recurring theme of "Little people can do big things too." The fact is that it is in the little things of life that we are transformed. Our transformation takes place not because we deserve it or because we did something great; rather, it takes place because we were faithful to the will of God in our lives.

Some people are called to be presidents or popes and leaders of big things. Some people are called to be renowned doctors who save lives on a daily basis. Some people are called to face danger, fight wars, and end terrible conflicts. There are many ways to fulfill God's commands but only one way to fulfill God's will and that is to listen to His voice in your own personal life. If God is calling you to be a stay at home mom and make three plus meals a day, handle loads of laundry and do the hundred and one things necessary to be a good mother and wife, then that is where your sanctification will arise. And that is where your fortitude will be tested. Sometimes we fail at things not so much because we are weak and have little fortitude but rather because we are not doing what we are supposed to be doing.

Courage can come in a myriad of forms and it can be difficult to see the value of courage in doing little tasks well. Bearing adversity with courage can mean getting up in the morning and taking care of your family during the flu season. Facing a classroom of kids who are not all angels (and with some, in fact, who are doing a fair imitation of scenes out of *The Exorcist*) may require more fortitude than the warrior who goes into battle. The office worker, the truck driver, the carpenter, the merchant, everyone has those times when great strength of character is demanded even in the little daily acts of our ordinary duties. We have to face choices all day long, the same choices Eowyn faced, to be strong and drive back the evil that is assaulting us or to turn away and let evil have its way.

Sad to say, but Eowyn did not have a great example in her Uncle Théoden. Granted, he came out from under the evil spell that Wormtongue had placed on him; but for a time great harm had been done because he had not shown the fortitude he ought to have. He allowed himself to be brainwashed into a dark and helpless state where he had become the tool of Saruman. He simply did not fight back hard enough against the whispers of evil which assailed his brain. Isn't that the way with us also? Usually it is not the great times of trial that cost us our position of strength but rather it is when we are tired and little things mount up. Words are whispered that shake our confidence and a sarcastic remark may make us think unjustified thoughts about another. How often the intonation of a simple remark can change our thinking, and we are left with a negative impression that we look to justify when there was nothing more to it than the unworthy comment of a thoughtless mind. "Oh, sure, he'll help you! We all know how helpful he can be!" Now you are certain that no help will come from that quarter and your resentment builds. Why is it that sarcasm seems to hold more weight than the truth itself? Perhaps because sarcasm seems so sure of itself whereas the truth tends to be a bit confusing at times and wavers between extremes. We like to take sides, and we like to be sure of ourselves so a smart remark can mean a lot to us even though it should not.

Théoden's lack of fortitude allowed a quick-tongued, smart-aleck to rule his judgment. We saw the living death that it offered. Contrast Wormtongue's twisted rebuttal to Gandalf's valiant attempt to warn Theoden calling him "…carrion-fowl that grows fat on war." Without fortitude to protect our healthy nature, we are led into the madness of evil reasoning.

Television is often the source of quick, smart remarks that tend to dictate the morals of our country. Some of those lessons in morality may have some validity but others most certainly do not! How is it that talk show hosts and news commentators become the voice of reason when they may have little training or experience in listening to the Voice of Reason? Should a person perhaps believe in God, the foundation of all wisdom, and pray and have a close relationship with the Lord before giving out advice? Does it matter if we think of God at all? Where does fortitude come from in the first place? Since there is a God and we are called to serve Him and He offers us the virtues to accomplish His will, then does it make sense that we spend so much time listening to those who never mention His name or care for His will?

If we lack the necessary fortitude, we may be graced with someone who can help us get back on track as Theoden experienced a metamorphosis through the guidance Gandalf. But we must do our part and at least try to keep our strength of mind so that we can bear adversity well. We must ask God for His help, and we must be prepared to admit when we are off track and do all we can to straighten our course. As with any virtue it will only work when it is in tune with the song of the Creator.

When Eowyn faced the Nazgul King, she unveiled the fortitude that she had been gifted with. It was her very strength of character combined with her endowed womanly nature which undid the almost overpowering evil before her. When the king of the Nazgul comes to threaten our well-being or that of a loved one, it is best to be prepared. Only in our faithfulness to God, who is infinitely more powerful than any evil force, can we ever hope to gain the fortitude necessary to fight the battles of our lives be they big or little.

Temperance

> " 'It is a gift that I bring you from the Lady of Rivendell,' answered Halbarad. 'She wrought it in secret, and long was the making. But she also sends word to you: The days now are short. Either our hope cometh, or all hope ends. Therefore I send thee what I have made for thee. Fare well, Elstone!'
>
> "And Aragorn said: 'Now I know what you bear. Bear it still for me awhile!' And he turned and looked away to the North under the great stars, and then he fell silent and spoke no more while the night's journey lasted." (The Return of the King)

Temperance is so often thought of in connection to the use of alcohol that it might be good to once again look in *Merriam-Webster's Collegiate Dictionary* and find the exact definition. The first definition is rather vague, "moderation in action, thought or feeling: restraint,"; but the second definition seems more to the point, "habitual moderation in the indulgence of the appetites or passions,". Which character demonstrated this virtue to the point of excellence? Again there could be several candidates, but I would like to examine Aragorn since he, above anyone else, had to moderate his own natural response to the call to greatness and maintain for a time the figure of a hidden king in the form of a simple though mysterious ranger.

Aragorn not only had to moderate his appetite in a physical way in that he had to live for years as a virtual outcast who roamed the whole countryside keeping the land as safe as he could manage with his few assistants in the Dunedain of the north, he also had to control his passion for the woman that he loved, Arwen, for he had many important tasks to accomplish before he could set his mind to matters of marriage and personal happiness. Here we have a character who does the complete opposite of what modern television and romance novels would convince us is our right, namely to speak our minds, express our feelings, satisfy our appetites, and fulfill our passions. We are led to believe, in our own time, that greatness lies in being true to ourselves and in the imperative of meeting our personal needs even when they are simply strong wants. We are given the impression that we will need serious therapy if we suppress our inner urges and do not properly communicate our feelings. How ironic that the character who is the symbol of the hidden king is one of great restraint and self-control. The argument could be made that through this character we glimpse a world counter to our own, where the virtue of temperance sets us free to become the great persons that we are called to be.

It is not in exposing ourselves that we determine our full nature but rather it is in controlling ourselves enough to allow our personhood to be shaped and transformed by the greatest personality there is. After all, if we refuse the role of servant to the Most High, then how can we do His job and be called forth into the light of our full potential? We cannot be both the potter and the clay. If we decide we want to do things our own way and fulfill our desires then we are in fact abdicating the greater part of our existence. We are to listen to the voice of God and that means we can't be forever talking. We have to obey and that means we can't be forever refusing the challenges that make us tired and uncomfortable. We have to put aside our appetites and not grow fat because it is a matter of simple self-discipline to refuse to buy and eat everything we want and to stuff ourselves at every meal. We are not called as children of God to indulge in our many passions that keep us momentarily happy by convincing ourselves that this dress, these computer games, our next vacation, a nicer car, a better house, and all the rest will fill our empty spaces and enliven our meaningless existence. Aragorn was truly a king because he did what few men before him, and even of his time, would do. He controlled himself, and he did not give in to temptations. It is not a mere coincidence that temperance and temptations are such similar words.

Robert Foster in his concordance for *The Lord of the Rings* makes his point abundantly clear when he explains the history of the Dunedain by saying, "The purity of the Dunedain blood was lessened by intermarriage with lesser Men, especially the Northmen, and more importantly, by sloth and love of luxury." Lesser men! What an honest appraisal of those who allow themselves to be ruled by their appetites. Aragorn could have chosen the same path of his ancestors. In fact it was the virtue of humility that restrained his pride from thinking that he deserved to be recognized as the heir of Isildur before his time. He could see himself making the same mistakes that those before him had made. He was not blind to his weaknesses. Because he knew this truth about himself he did a very smart thing. He would not allow himself to be put in the way of temptation. It took the combined efforts of Gandalf and Elrond to bring him forth to face his destiny as a revealed king.

I hate to pick on Denethor, but he is a perfect example of one who did not control his passions. His life was ruled by them and his death was arranged by them. But there is an even more poignant character in his son, Boromir, in that he was so close to being a temperate man, but he allowed himself to be swayed not so much by his personal ambition but from the habit of ambition he had learned from his father. His fall was so terribly sad because he was so much closer to the full realization of his being in that he had so many good and noble characteristics, which had been developed through the virtue of temperance. He was a man who did as his father bade him and worked hard no matter how difficult the circumstances. We can easily imagine that Boromir would stay at his post when lesser men fled and that he would forgo the pleasures of wining and dining if his position demanded it. It was only after he had succumbed to temptation that he made the greatest mistake of his life; he attempted to take what was not his and grab hold of an evil power which would have destroyed him. Boromir would have almost certainly witnessed many good examples in his life time, but his father, who should have been his greatest guide to what is virtuous, lead him astray and pointed the way to personal destruction.

Our Lord Jesus Christ does not mince words when it comes to such a situation. He says, "But he that shall scandalize one of these little ones that believe in me, it were better for him that a millstone should be hanged about his neck, and that he should be drowned in the depth of the sea." {Matt. Xviii.10} Who is the little one? Anyone in our care and that may be our grandchild or a neighbor's teenager or our infant son. And how do we choose among the many examples in our lives? We look to the Master and see who is most in accordance with His truth. Many of us have had the experience of having parents or figures of authority that were not good examples, and we had to find a way to deal with these people while choosing not to follow them. That decision often costs a great deal because we are forced to declare our allegiance to the Hidden King and not to the powers that exist on the Earth.

It is especially sad when the person who tries to tempt us to sin is the very person who should most help led us to a life of virtue. Unfortunately, because of the loss of the sense of virtue and sin, there are many families in which neither the father nor the mother can honestly say that they are walking in the light of Christ or that they even understand what they are called to be or do in the sight of the Most High. Thus we have children who are being led around in a whirlwind of activity from sports to music lessons to after-school programs to crafts to family gatherings; and since there are multiple marriages, each child can experience a multitude of Thanksgivings, Christmases, and Easters every year. Or, more accurately, they can experience a multitude of parties where God may be given the name of the day but is hardly thought of beyond that point. Morality and virtue are downgraded to the mere opinion of what one feels at a certain point in life.

Where is there room to think, much less prepare oneself to avoid the occasion of sin? Where is there time to appreciate the traditions of our culture? Is it all about food and television specials? Where is the space to experience the religious practices as anything other than, "one more thing to do"? We walk right into sinful situations because we are so busy we don't even see where we are going. And our little ones? They hardly know what their lives are about much less what self-discipline and control mean because their whole lives are a forced march from one activity or food station to another. One could say they have to be disciplined to keep so busy; but that is hardly what Aragorn stood for. His life was one of meaning, in which he learned slowly of his mission, and he attempted to fulfill each labor to the best of his ability. He did not know what the future would bring and he did not rush around trying to solve everyone's problems or do more than he was capable of doing. He did few things and he did them well. Granted he may have been extremely busy at times, but he was not trying to be other than himself. His life was one of chosen service, not a series of imposed duties.

How can we exercise this virtue of temperance in our own lives? Perhaps it is a matter of prioritizing the activities of our day according to those which do the most to bring us closer to God. It may be that there are things you feel you should be doing but you have no real reason why. You had baseball practice three times a week when you were a kid and you simply think it would be unfair to deprive your child of the same experience. But the question is; does that activity call forth our relationship with God? It may. It may not. You may look at everything and say with growing despair that everything can bring us closer to God and thus you can't justify eliminating anything from your schedule. Consider the issue of prioritizing. Some things are less important than other things though we may have strong emotional ties to them. Only God can demand our greatest loyalty.

We are human and we simply can't be rushing madly about all the time without it costing us something. Why are we rushing? Do we think our life has no meaning if we are still for a time? Are we avoiding an encounter with the voice of God? We need time to pray. Temptations hit us when we are unprepared and unable to see what is right in front of us. Prayer is an antidote to that problem. Every human being needs to speak to God every day. That is how one gets to know God, and that is how we gain the grace to practice the virtues, and that is where we learn to recognize temptations and avoid them.

Did Aragorn pray? Did he go off by himself in a quiet place and think or ponder the great issues of his time? In prayer, he would be able to rise above his weak, human nature and consider the great task that had been appointed to him. We too have many tasks appointed to us and we can accomplish them. But we must allow ourselves the opportunity to be filled and refreshed by the Spirit of Him who governs all things. We must use our will to resist temptations and exercise our self-discipline in the noble virtue of temperance.

Chapter Three
Gifts From On High

"Tolkien cast his mythology in this form because he wanted it to be remote and strange, and yet at the same time not to be a lie. He wanted the mythological and legendary stories to express his own moral view of the universe; and as a Christian he could not place this view in a cosmos without the God that he worshipped." (J.R.R. Tolkien: A biography by Humphrey Carpenter p. 99)

In the teachings of the Church, we have come to understand that the Holy Spirit works in our lives in a very tangible way. We gain much through the grace of the Holy Spirit in our lives. As *The New Saint Joseph Baltimore Catechism* states, "The gifts of the Holy Spirit enable us to catch the breath of the Holy Spirit, moving the ship of our soul much faster and farther than we could ever sail it by using the virtues ourselves." In other words, the Holy Spirit facilitates a better use and experience of the virtues, and they are exercised to a higher degree when the Holy Spirit helps us. We cannot go around ordering up the Holy Spirit like some computer expert who can help us increase our expertise, but we certainly can call on the Holy Spirit and ask for assistance. What the Holy Spirit will do is according to His will. He moves like the wind when and where He wants; and we have no place making demands on Him. Lest you lose heart, it may relieve you to know that Jesus promised His help on the day of His ascension. The help He has given is beyond words or categories, but the Church helps us understand the working of these gifts by naming seven of them. If we look at these gifts, we may come to see that not only has the Holy Spirit been alive and well in Middle-earth, but we have had more help on this Earth than perhaps we had ever realized.

Wisdom

" 'I am not made for perilous quests. I wish I had never seen the Ring! Why did it come to me? Why was I chosen?'

'Such questions cannot be answered,' said Gandalf. 'You may be sure that it was not for any merit that others do not possess; not for power or wisdom at any rate. But you have been chosen, and you must therefore use such strength and heart and wits as you have.'" (The Fellowship of the Ring)

Wisdom is the first gift of the Holy Spirit, and it helps us to judge correctly things concerning God. (Isaiah 11) As *The Saint Joseph Baltimore Catechism* says, "God is love and the Holy Spirit gives the wisdom of love to appreciate divine things, even crosses and tribulations." We find that in *The Lord of the Rings* it was Gandalf to whom everyone turned for wisdom. He was the one who could enlighten others about their path and how to best handle many situations. Unfortunately there were those who needed his wisdom but were reluctant to take it. As usual those who are truly wise are often misunderstood and underappreciated. Gandalf certainly had an extraordinary level of wisdom and because of that he was needed and cherished by those who understood him. In the movie, we are led to believe he avoided the path under the mountain which led to the Balrog, but in the book we read about a man who sees the inevitability of that path and the challenge he must face. He did not love the thought of the struggle that faced him in the murky depths, but he did see that which no one else could: a purpose and eventual purification, which we as readers and the other characters could not see. One gets the idea that Gandalf said yes to the fight with the Balrog long before he even went into the mountain. He knew that there was more to many experiences of life than meet the eye.

My mistake with Gandalf was to think of him as simply an amazing character that did wonderful things which no one else could do. But after reading about the gifts of the Holy Spirit, I was reminded of the role of God in the intimate movements of our daily lives. God will help us and give us gifts which surpass anything we could have imagined. Was Gandalf a magical figure who had supernatural powers in order to make the story interesting? It could be as simple as that. But somehow that train of thought seems to diminish the greatness of the story which leads us towards something much better than just a good tale. Gandalf could have been the conduit through which the Holy Spirit was working in order to accomplish a divine mission.

Gandalf could have refused this role and turned toward evil as Saruman did or he could have insisted on staying in his quiet little realm doing only what was asked of him in grave necessity as the Brown Wizard did. But Gandalf gave a continuous "yes" to all that was asked of him and for this he was given great gifts to help him meet the challenges which faced him. It was in his "yes" even to the mines of Moria that he met the deadly evil of the Balrog in which he found himself facing utter destruction and later became transformed into Gandalf the White, who was greater and more powerful than his enemy Saruman, who had once been greater than himself.

To leap forward into a new level of greatness is not something we can make happen even if we do buy the right lottery ticket or land the best job or even make an outstanding marriage. The greatness and power necessary to do God's will is not something we can make happen. We can humbly pray to do His will, but we may find that His will for us is simply to do the laundry today, and we haven't been able to do that particularly well. We may blame the broken washing machine or the pen which leaked or the detergent which hardly got the whites white. But the point is that greatness lies not in the eyes of this world but in the mystery of God's will for us and our willingness to carry that out despite difficulties. He may be giving us abundant gifts to do all sort of things, which we fail to realize the significance of because they seem so ordinary. For example, you may have had a really bad day at the office, but the soup you brought to your sick neighbor helped him more than words could say and, in fact, you were an answer to a silent prayer. You may pray day and night for the relief of a loved one who continues to suffer, and you cannot understand why the good and compassionate Master sees fit to allow your family member to suffer and seems to refuse to hear one iota of your prayer, yet the redemption going on inside that soul could be very great. Your own soul which may have been formerly self-absorbed could now become much more open to the grace of God in receiving and transmitting His love. The gift of wisdom is not so much about us using God's gifts as it is about us being transformed by His gifts. As we encounter God and in His wisdom, we see His presence in everything as He really exists, then we too become wise and pass that gift along without the least bit of pride because we know, above all, that we are not the givers of gifts, but the couriers of His magnificence in the kingdom of our present Earth.

Understanding

" 'Would that the Lady had given us a light, such a gift as she gave to Frodo!'

'It will be more needed where it is bestowed,' said Aragorn. 'With him lies the true Quest. Ours is but a small matter in the great deeds of this time. A vain pursuit from its beginning, maybe, which no choice of mine can mar or mend. Well, I have chosen. So let us use the time as best we may!" (The Two Towers)

The gift of understanding is not simply a copy of wisdom but it really is a separate gift unto itself. "Understanding gives us insight into the mysteries of faith so that we may live by them." (*The New Saint Joseph Baltimore Catechism*) In wisdom, we judge correctly things concerning God. When we understand things, we gain special insight into issues that are a mystery to others. For example, Gandalf was wise when he recognized that Frodo was meant to have the ring, and he had understanding when he was able to gently counsel Pippin as they faced the possibility of their death in Gondor. Many times Gandalf acted as a friend who understood the hearts of those around him and how to best lead them towards their mission, the love of the greater good. He could lead others past the pain and suffering of the present moment to strengthen their limbs and souls to do the tasks which were set before them.

Maxmilian Kolbe was a real person who had the gifts of wisdom and understanding. While he was in a concentration camp, he was able to do extraordinary good, which would normally be beyond the level of even the most ardent soul without the assistance of the supernatural strength of the Holy Spirit. He was able to offer up his meager rations to other men who he saw needed the support of such a bit of human kindness though he too was starving. He talked men out of committing suicide. He was able to hold religious ceremonies, even hearing confessions and celebrating the Mass under circumstances that should have made such acts quite impossible. His ability to see God even in the midst of such a place as a Nazi concentration camp speaks of one who was being touched directly by the hand of God. The fact that he not only maintained his faith but grew in his faith, and turned others away from despair to acts of virtue and faith, show that he had understanding beyond the lot of most men.

Again, we cannot demand understanding, but perhaps we have experienced this gift more than we had realized. There may have been times when we have faced a person who was suffering great sorrow and we found words to help, and later as we reflected on the experience we honestly could not take credit for our sudden burst of insight. "I don't know what came over me, but I said just the right thing!" We should be very grateful when that happens, for we have all had the opposite experience, in which we think we will come up with a witty remark or a kind platitude, and we find that we have done more harm than good. We may have practiced a little speech or a response to a particular situation only to fall flat on our faces. We wonder why. What went wrong? Perhaps we were relying on our own human nature too much and not calling on God enough. Think about the experience of Frodo, Pippin, and Merry at the Prancing Pony. Remember Frodo's true name being accidentally revealed? When someone forgets what their mission is and the importance of it, even for a short time, then mistakes are made. Understanding happens when we pray for it, and the Holy Spirit sees fit to give us this grace.

Counsel

" 'In this evil hour I have come on an errand over many dangerous leagues to Elrond: a hundred and ten days I have journeyed all alone. But I do not seek allies in war. The might of Elrond is in wisdom not in weapons, it is said. I come to ask for counsel and the unraveling of hard words.' " (The Fellowship of the Ring)

We hear of counselors all the time and thus we think that good counsel is ours for the asking. After all there are school counselors for our kids, and counselors at many job sites, and if there is ever a disaster, the government will send out counselors to help us through the rough times. So we feel fairly safe that this is one of those gifts we have been given in abundance, and therefore we don't need to say too much on this matter. Actually, there is a difference between the counsel of men and the counsel of God. When we receive the gift of counsel from the Holy Spirit, we may not be as popular as when we give the counsel repeated by many well-intentioned but less-informed mortals. One must remember that God's thoughts are often different from man's thoughts and so we tend to meet the unexpected when faced with good counsel from on High.

Legolas was a good counselor who often tried quietly to give information and insight according to his long range vision. He could see what others could not. We may have experiences where we heard a whisper in our heart telling us to take a different road literally or figuratively, and at the time we could not exactly understand why but later we were extremely glad we had changed course for there was an unforeseen danger that lay directly in our path. Some would say that we simply listened to an intuition from our own minds that correctly diverted us from danger. It could be. It could also be that we are not alone and that God has done what He said and given us each an angel to guide and protect us and that we are often the receivers of unrealized assistance, but in our arrogance, we insist that we have done everything for ourselves.

The counsel of the world will often assure us that we have rights and needs and that we should take good care of ourselves or we will be no use to anyone. But the counsel of God is primarily concerned with the salvation of our souls, so we may not be advised according to our personal preferences. For example, when we were young it is possible that our mother might have told us not to eat too much candy and instead offer up our extra money to the poor. Good old Mom was trying to do several good things for us though at the time we hardly appreciated it. She probably wanted to spare us and herself the extra trip to the dentist for those nasty fillings, and she probably wanted to avoid the problems related with being overweight and also she probably hoped on some higher plane that we might think about becoming self-disciplined because, frankly, it is good for our souls to avoid being self-indulgent. Maybe, if she is approaching sainthood, she even hoped that we might come to realize that sacrifice can be a source of redemption for ourselves and others. Perhaps we could even be led to the highest point of human existence through this simple offering, to experience a sincere love of God as the author of all good. Mother just asked us to do one simple thing, but there are many possible ramifications of this one piece of good counsel.

We are offered the daily crosses of work, noise, and trouble and not having enough time to do all the things we are supposed to do and then we hear these whispered comments, "Don't lose your cool. Be patient with this very annoying person. Smile. Try again. Pray. Don't give up." Legolas, Gandalf, and Aragorn all had the gift of giving good counsel. They all offered advice that led to something better, and they all knew that what they were about was more important than the petty, selfish interests of the moment so they were unabashed at giving their advice.

What happens when we repeatedly refuse to listen to the good counsel offered to us through-out the day and through-out our lives? It is said that the path to hell is hell, and the path to heaven is heaven. Denethor would not listen to the counsel Gandalf offered and he despaired and burned himself to death. That was a very dramatic vision of one choosing the fires of hell rather than his humble role as steward. Saruman would not accept the gift of good counsel that Gandalf tried to offer him. He chose a twisted path of deceit, destruction and death.

In our culture today there is an assessment that we live in a "secular and materialistic" society. Secular means that we are concerned about life on Earth in this mortal state while materialistic means we are over-anxious about the "stuff" in our lives. So basically, we are classified as a culture that is concerned with things of this world. How then do we receive counsel from the Holy Spirit that directs us away from things of this world towards the salvation of our soul in the world to come? Often it seems that we are so inundated with worldly advice that we can't even hear the quiet working of our own soul much less the voice of the Holy Spirit. But say we are trying to pray, and we are thinking about our job and our mortgage and our kids and how we want to get out of debt and how our kids aren't doing so great in school, but we aren't sure whose fault that is. So we ponder, and we pray for understanding and some good counsel. We hear nothing. We sit there and wait and listen and still all we can discern is a rumbling in our tummy and the sound of kids who are not going to be put off much longer. Counsel, where are you? Eventually we have to get up and get to the duties of parenting and perhaps get a little reading in before bed. We read a fascinating book with a wonderfully noble character and though we admire him greatly we think how it hardly applies to our world today. One can't go around giving up our stable life styles. It just isn't done. So we go to sleep. We need a good night's sleep. But we wake up in the middle of the night and there is the beginning of this thought that is bothering us. Part of the reason our kids might not be doing so well in school is because they have some discipline issues. We also realize that we haven't balanced the checkbook in a very long time and that we are spending more than we make. And to make matters worse, our spouse is having a hard time at work, and we haven't talked about it because we have been so busy. Everyone seems angry, and we don't even know why exactly. We need to make some changes but what and how is a frustrating muddle. It is the middle of the night. Worldly counsel says to go back to sleep and deal with the issue later when one is well rested. But in the day there is never time. A quiet voice begins to offer suggestions. They are wild, crazy ideas about cutting down on extra-curricular activities and having the kids help out more at home and perhaps even home tutoring! You are feeling dizzy! No one can ask more of you! No one expects you to give up your job and spend more time with the kids and perhaps help out the spouse with the report he has to write. And give up the extra car? Why, it would be like going back to the stone-age!

But the thoughts are there and there are some workable notions among them. But they would require sacrifice and dedication to something higher than anything one can see with mortal eyes. Perhaps our child is not called to go to medical school, and he has a vocation to something much different than we ever expected. Perhaps we have a vocation too. Perhaps our lives are a religious experience in which we encounter the mystery of God every day. Perhaps the counsel we receive only sounds strange to our ears because we are so used to the world's way of doing things, and we are simply in the habit of following secular, materialistic thinking.

The nice thing for us is that we are not made of stone. Our time of choosing is not over. As long as the good Lord has mercy on us and keeps our hearts beating then we carry within our soul the possibility of redemption which is a change for the better. We are never done being transformed by God's grace and lucky for us we are never abandoned to the world and all its false gods of personal comfort and pleasure. Our lives are not about the pursuit of happiness unless you realize that happiness can only be found in the embrace of the Divine Will. There is the best counsel of all.

Fortitude

" 'But last night I told you of Sauron the Great, the Dark Lord... Always after a defeat and a respite, the Shadow takes another shape and grows again.'

'I wish it need not have happened in my time,' said Frodo.

'So do I,' said Gandalf, 'and so do all who live to see such times. But that is not for them to decide. All we have to decide is what to do with the time that is given us.'" (The Fellowship of the Ring)

"Fortitude is the moral virtue that ensures firmness in difficulties and constancy in the pursuit of the good. It strengthens the resolve to resist temptations and to overcome obstacles in the moral life." (*The Catechism of the Catholic Church* 1808) We already did this one, you say? We covered the virtue of fortitude and that is saying a lot but that is not completely the same as the gift of fortitude. As with counsel, we may be lucky enough to receive it from On High and then we pass it along; but with fortitude it gets even more exciting.

A martyr is a person who surrenders his life in order to witness to the truth of their faith in God. Some of the martyrs suffered unbelievable cruelty at the hands of others and yet they would not recant. What they did was beyond human strength. To serve God means being open to His grace and that grace gives us strength in big and little ways. Not too many people are called upon to be martyrs in blood though there have been more people to die for their faith in the last hundred years than in all of history before. We have lived in a time of great choosing and more people have made the ultimate sacrifice of their lives rather than say or do anything which might offend God. China has known years of public and private persecution that have forced the believers in Christ into an underground where they suffer daily for their faith in ways we in a free country cannot imagine. Pretty much all of communism was a virulent attack on the faith of Christianity, and millions have died professing their love of Jesus Christ. In the Middle East in our own time, we have watched horrified once again by attacks on innocent people who have done nothing more than profess to be followers of Christ. Fortitude was and always has been a serious gift of the Holy Spirit.

In *The Lord of the Rings* one can only wonder at the strength of Frodo to carry on when he was well beyond all strength. How could Sam offer up his own water when he was thirsty beyond anything he had ever experienced knowing he could surely die? Gandalf receives fortitude to face and eventually defeat the Balrog. We all know that we would not like to be in his shoes and if we imagine that we could handle such a situation coolly, well, we are probably fooling ourselves. It tends to be shortly after we have been enjoying a good fantasy about personal domination over evil when a real evil comes to face us and we find ourselves sliding to the floor in a faint. Look at Gimli when he is faced with the paths of the dead. He had always been quite assured of his own fortitude and thus he is amazed when he is terrified of the path leading to the dead. Legolas is not afraid and it is in the leadership of his friend that Gimli is pulled forward. Sometimes our friends and loved ones can play that role for us in leading us where our hearts are loath to go. They act as instruments of fortitude for us and help us over the hard parts.

It is no wonder then that the world esteems strength but sees as foolish the strength given by God, for often when we are gifted with fortitude we are going against the very trends of our times. It takes great fortitude to keep a life growing inside of you when someone advises you to have an abortion. It takes fortitude to pull out of a conversation because it is impure. It takes fortitude to refuse a job that you need because it involves a shady deal. It takes fortitude to train yourself to refrain from using bad words and losing your temper. It takes fortitude to pray every day, even when you are sick and behind schedule. It takes great fortitude to face your sins and to make reparation. Fortitude comes in all shapes and sizes and it is a good thing that Frodo was strong enough to accept the gift of fortitude and that Sam was willing to carry both the ring and Frodo, relying on a gift of strength that actually made his burden light.

There is a saying that if good men do nothing then evil will conquer. When we look at the troubles of our times and the evils that prevail we may feel the flickering of despair for the whispered voice of the Holy Spirit asks the impossible, and we are not up to the tasks of the day. It can all seem rather overwhelming. Yet God has been offering His strength for thousands of years. We can read the life of Moses. God was asking him to lead His people away from the land they had always known and to go to a place where God would lead him; and all they had to rely on was Moses' word and the miracles God chose to offer. Moses was offered an impossible task. He begged that his brother Aaron be allowed to do the speaking. He seemed to think that Aaron was more smooth-tongued and could accomplish this mission better than himself. But God had chosen him and though Aaron was to help, he was not given the fortitude that Moses was. Remember Moses on the mountain diligently copying down the Ten Commandments while Aaron was down below having a party and making a molten calf to appease the people? God knew what the people were doing. He still does.

When He bestows new life in conception, he has not made a mistake. He is not unaware of the troubles that await the mother and child. He is not blind to our suffering. He just knows far better than we do what He can offer in the gift of fortitude. Mountains can be moved and lives can be changed. A soul is called forth by God to do great things. Our limits are caused by our own refusal to accept His strength. When we accept the gift of fortitude, we are accepting a form of God's love for us, and we are taking the next step in our transformation into children of God who belong with

Him forever and ever in Heaven. When we have to walk over the mountain passes, it is best not to look down, and when we have to scale the heights of difficulties, it is best not to look too far ahead. We must trust God and He will help us with the gift of fortitude.

Knowledge

"At last Frodo spoke with hesitation. 'I believed that you were a friend before the letter came,' he said, 'or at least I wished to. You have frightened me several times tonight, but never in the way that servants of the Enemy would, or so I imagine. I think one of his spies would – well, seem fairer and feel fouler, if you understand.'

'I see,' laughed Strider. 'I look foul and feel fair. Is that it? All that is gold does not glitter, not all those who wander are lost.'"
(The Fellowship of the Ring)

"To see God in all of creation and to praise Him accordingly and to realize our own nothingness so that we desire God alone." (*The New Saint Joseph Baltimore Catechism*) Where do we see that in *The Lord of the Rings*? In the person of Gandalf, we find a figure who seeks knowledge to do a great good or to protect the innocent from harm. In the person of Elrond, we find someone who is a master of wisdom. Galadriel is considered one of the noblest elves in Middle-earth for her part in opposing the evil of Morgoth and keeping her kingdom of Lorien safe from the destructive powers of Sauron while helping the ring bearer and his friends. She, like the others, had the wits to refuse to try to wield the deadly ring of power though they had power in their own right that was greater than most. Each of these figures was extraordinarily great and could have longed to be the greatest. But each of them realized that they were less than the greatest. Even though God is not so named in the trilogy, *The Lord of the Rings*, one comes to the inevitable conclusion that God is what really matters to all three of these characters.

In *The Silmarillion* there is the figure of Eru who is the Great Creator. He is God, so to speak, and all things must choose to be either in unison with him or in discord. Those that turn away from His song of creation become a source of great destruction and sorrow to those who try live in union with the Great Source of all Being. In all the great and noble figures of *The Lord of the Rings*—Gandalf, Bilbo, Frodo, Sam, Pippin, Merry, Aragorn, Legolas, Gimli, Eowyn, Galadriel, Elrond, Arwen, Theoden, Faramir, Treebeard, and several others—we find persons who recognize that they are not so terribly important, and they have a built-in sense of humility which allows them to truly know not only who they are but who the Creator really is. They may not be able to define the Great Being which rules over all things, but in their humility they know that which is most important; they know they are not He. That is the greatest piece of knowledge a person can have. It is the knowledge that can free a soul to truly fulfill its destiny in God's perfect plan. All other knowledge is of secondary importance because without this, one is forever trapped in a dead end maze which leads to pointless acts of destruction.

Saruman had a choice. He knew he was not God and yet he chose to accept another in the place of God. That was a deadly mistake. One cannot simply recognize that one is not God but then by one's own free choice and pleasure decide who should be God because to do so would be to claim God's power and place. Thus any false god is really a reflection of setting oneself up as a God-figure because one is refusing to recognize the truth of God and then choosing what god it pleases to worship. It takes a lot of pride to take such a step. Even under the guise of worshiping and serving another, we are really serving ourselves.

Let us take a look at the false gods we claim as our own. Many people see fit to work very hard, even to the point of missing or ignoring any church services or any personal time to pray to the One above. The claim is that they are just taking care of their family and that it is necessary to do so in this world. When we speak of the gift of knowledge we are talking about a conviction that we know something to be true and that our actions should reflect that belief. If we have knowledge of the existence of God but do not involve ourselves in worship on a community level, and we spend little personal time thinking, thanking, praising and pondering God, then we are living a lie. To know and yet to live as if we do not know is insane. It leads us away from the noble fruits that each of the characters I mentioned before reflected. To be great as a human being requires that we accept God's primacy and act on that knowledge. All things will work out in consequence of that right ordering of our souls. For it is truly better to lose your life in this world and gain your soul, than to save your life in this world and lose your soul.

One thinks, "Yes, this all sounds good, but my reality means my kids need money for school and I have to work and I get so tired that prayer time gets pushed aside. I mean to pray and I want to do better, but the good Lord isn't helping me very much. He must understand what I am going through. He is a merciful God so He can't demand what I simply can't give." The problem with this line of thinking is that we are simply excusing our failure rather than asking God to help us do what appears to be the impossible. The fact is that we simply don't want to pay the high price of acting on our knowledge of God. We want to believe that simply believing in God is enough and that will see us through into the next world. The problem here is that the devil also believes in God but he simply refuses to obey Him. Who wants to follow his example?

So, God does ask us to do the unthinkable and leave a job that destroys our prayer life? Does God want us to skip sleep and stick to a prayer life even when we are terribly tired? Does God ask us to put our child's happiness after Him? Our boy can't play sports because it breaks up family time? Our girl can't act in the school play because issues of modesty and making oneself an object of temptation? We can't decide for ourselves when it is time for us to die? We can't decide for ourselves when a baby becomes human? We can't do whatever we want in the pursuit of scientific knowledge because God is offended by the destruction of human life even at its earliest stages of development? Who is this God who dares to demand so much of us? There is the gift of knowledge! The Holy Spirit offers it to whom He will.

Piety

"Perhaps the imaginary account of a typical day tells us something in that it starts with a journey to mass at St. Aloysius'; and any close scrutiny of his life must take account of the importance of his religion. His commitment to Christianity and particular to the Catholic Church was total." (J.R.R. Tolkien: A biography by Humphrey Carpenter p. 133)

Piety is an expression of our love for God. But it also involves love of those who share this love of God. We call those people saints. To love a saint and to recognize their goodness is to love God by extension. Also, to love, to do acts of prayer, formal worship, and quiet acts of devotion, is to exhibit the gift of piety. There simply are not a lot of obvious acts of piety in *The Lord of the Rings*. Tolkien made it clear that he did not want his work to be didactic, forcing the mind to accept his claims of morality. Rather, he leads the mind on a journey that rather beautifully reflects the journeys of life in all its myriad turns and twists, and yet, through the nobility or corruption of his characters, one sees not only the hand of God, but also the spirit of the communion of saints. But he does not want to paint too clear a picture, because God is a mystery, and a good story does not completely unlock a mystery, but rather helps us gain insight. The human mind is not able to grasp supernatural things on a surface level but can ruminate upon our experience of God on a hidden level. I think that is why Tolkien kept the word of God hidden and why he shows so little in the way of worship or piety.

Tolkien was an ardent Catholic. His mother was a convert who suffered much for her conversion and through her he learned to accept the suffering of the soul in love with God. It is part of our human experience on Earth to suffer, and suffering is only redeemed in that we can offer our pain to God. It is He alone that gives meaning and purpose to our existence despite and perhaps because of our terrible suffering. We are drawn to One who is so great and majestic that we realize that, no matter how much we have suffered, He knows more about trouble than we ever will. We are forced into a position where we must express our love, our need, our gratitude, and our hope to Him alone who can hear, understand, and answer us.

In *The Lord of the Rings,* we would have to stretch our imaginations a bit to see the unspoken parts, but it would not be a long stretch to believe that Bilbo went to some kind of church, or that Gandalf and Aragorn prayed in the lonely moments of the dark night, or that Galadriel and Arwen worshipped God in common, traditional rituals. If we were able to climb into the book and actually go and visit Middle-earth, one would expect to see some church spires in the distance and one could clearly see Sam dressed in his Sunday best. It would all seem so right and natural. There would be a terrible vacuum if one went to Middle-earth and all visible signs of worship were missing. No holy statues or pictures? No holidays based on ancient traditions of worship? No baptism? No marriage ceremony asking the blessing of God? No confessing of guilt and relief from mortal sin? No last rites for the dying? No public, common prayer? No, it would not be Middle-earth. It would be some place not related to Earth at all. It would not know man. It would not know God. It could not exist as a good place in our souls.

There is the belief going back to the ancient Israelites that the hand of God's wrath is stayed by the prayers of a few faithful. We think of Noah, Abraham, and Moses. In Noah's time, God wiped out the world but for a remnant; but he said he would not do that again. When the Angel of God was going to wipe out Sodom and Gomorrah, it was Abraham who begged for the lives of the people, even bargaining that if there were only ten good men the cities would be saved. Unfortunately ten good men could not be found, and once again the remnant had to flee. Then with

Moses, God is hot again against those who have disregarded His commands. Remember Aaron and the Golden Calf? Here it is Moses who pleads for the lives of his people and persuades the Good Lord to have mercy on the remnants who are fleeing from slavery in Egypt. There are other examples but the pattern is the same. A holy person prays to save others who have stirred the wrath of God.

When we pray, not only do we love God, but we also extend that love out to the whole world. Prayer matters; and it has incredible power that even the one praying cannot realize this side of Heaven. Piety is an act of love primarily; but it is also an act of obedience where we do what our soul is commanded to do when we acknowledge the truth of God. We are human and we need to express our love, devotion and obedience in a concrete way. It is not enough for us mortals to hint at it as Tolkien does in *The Lord of the Rings*. Our souls would starve on such a diet. We need concrete pictures, words, songs, rituals, traditions, and sacraments which put us directly in touch with the living God. We cannot hope to reach God on our own by giving him our leftover bit of time. Our arms are not long enough to reach Him. But God comes down to us, and we are blessed with a church that enables us to better know, love, and serve the Lord. Our greatest journey may begin by crossing the threshold into church. It is there we pray as a community to become what God calls us all to be. It is there that we touch the spiritual world of angels and saints in a very special way. Piety is pure gift.

Fear of the Lord

*" 'But fear no more! I would not take this thing, if it lay by the highway. Not were Minas Tirith falling in ruin and I alone could save her, so, using the weapon of the Dark Lord for her good and my glory. No, I do not wish for such triumphs, Frodo, son of Drogo... I love only that which they defend: the city of the men of Numenor and I would have her loved for her memory, her ancientry, her beauty, and her present wisdom. Not feared, save as men may fear the dignity of a man, old and wise.' "
(The Two Towers)*

Fear is generally not considered a good thing. The devil does his utmost to inspire fear and despair in our souls. We are to fear sin. We are to fear evil. But should we ever fear God when He is all good and loves us even unto His death on the cross? There is a time when Gandalf is faced with a choice on the top of the tower of Orthanc. He had suffered greatly at the hands of Saruman. Yet, when it came down to it there was One whom he feared to offend more. There was an understanding in Gandalf's mind which reached deeply. He told Saruman that, given the choice between the Dark Lord or Saruman, he would serve neither, even though that meant punishment and death. As we know, he was saved; but the choice was made before he knew he could be saved. His rescue seems in part to be in some way connected to his commitment to serve the Unseen that rules over all. He had made a commitment to something that could best be described as Goodness itself and a complete rejection of evil.

Aragorn was afraid of something, though it is never exactly spelled out. He is afraid of failing to be better than his forefathers who had grabbed at the power of the ring and created a cycle of exile and doom. Who is he afraid of failing exactly? Later, why does he accept the challenge to take on that very role he had so long refused? I think the answer in both cases is the same. He refused out of fear of his mortal weakness and tendency toward sin. He knew that he was not ready, and he dared not make the same offense as which his forefather had made. Later, he accepts the chance that is offered; because it is clear that that is what is expected of him and it is necessary for the safety and stability of those he loves to do so. He is obedient to a Higher Power in both respects. He fears not to be obedient. He trusts that his obedience will save him.

Frodo was not given an order, but he knew all too well that he had a call which only he could answer. He knew, deep into the recesses of his being, that there was no escaping the trials which awaited him. His best hope lay in his obedience to the fate which was at his feet. He could have refused the burden set before him. It was not only his love of others that put strength into his fearful will but also the sure knowledge that something much greater than anything he could imagine was at work, and it was best not to refuse to do one's part. Even though he could not see himself succeeding, he thought it better to die in the effort than to refuse the challenge that awaited him. Life or death was not the overriding issue. Doing that which he was called to do was the focus.

With Sam, it seems that much of his wisdom is a sort of folk wisdom passed down from father to son, and that the Gaffer had contributed much to his formation. Somehow one gets a very comfortable and safe feeling with Sam; that he is standing on the bedrock of common sense. He likes to quote the witticisms of his old Gaffer and in this habit we see a boy who is devoted to his dad. We do not sense fear except the fear to hurt or offend. In this respect we find the closest thing to a holy fear of the Lord. It is right and good to avoid sin because we do not wish to offend the great power of God simply because justice will come upon us and punishment will be something terrible. It is the basis of logic to realize our own place in the universe and recognize that we are not the center. It is common sense to fear offending the

Ruler of the Universe. But it is Sam's love of his father that we should most wish to emulate. It is the love of a faithful child who sees the wisdom of his parent and does not want to fail to learn the lessons being offered. It is a sincere fear of hurting the One who is helping us. When one loves another, one does not want to ignore, reject or attack the one whom they love. Fear of failing to listen, to learn, to serve, and to return that love is the fear that animates the tired soul. Sam was exhausted many times and yet he went beyond his own Hobbit strength on the understanding that his Gaffer would not want him to give up. It was the bits of stories and family histories and tales of glory which prompted his heart and mind to make the great resolutions which helped him carry on despite the dark, cold, dangerous situations that he found himself in. We know in truth that the Gaffer was only an old man and he was not capable of the deeds that Sam achieved, yet Sam drew his strength from the vine that was firmly attached to the root which is the source of all life. In the story we trust Sam will become the source of much wisdom to his own children and, if they are as blessed as he, they will fear hurting him and ignoring his truth as we fear hurting our Father in heaven.

Chapter Four
The Rings of Power

> " 'A mortal, Frodo, who keeps one of the Great Rings, does not die, but he does not grow or obtain more life, he merely continues, until at last every minute is a weariness. And if he often uses the Ring to make himself invisible, he fades: he becomes in the end invisible permanently, and walks in the twilight under the eye of the dark power that rules the Rings. Yes, sooner or later— later, if he is strong or well-meaning to begin with, but neither strength nor good purpose will last—sooner or later, the dark power will devour him.'" (The Fellowship of the Ring)

The ring of power was a source of strength for the agents of evil. Do we have rings of power in our society today? Are there evil powers that can enslave us and use us so as to accomplish their fell ends? Do common objects in our cities, towns, and homes get hijacked for the very purpose of insidiously deceiving us by their utter common availability into thinking that they are not really dangerous? Do these objects become the tool of those evil forces which work to bring about the doom of a great many souls?

Not many people in our society today like to speak about God openly. There are too many different opinions and ways of offending someone. So it is best to keep God-centered conversations in the family or with a few close friends. At the same time there are not many people who feel comfortable speaking about the devil.

Few want to believe he exists and for those who know of his presence it can be a very frightening and painful topic. Many will acknowledge his existence, but few people want to pull him out of his holes and challenge his strong holds. There is no disputing the fact that there are powers in the universe which do great harm and that go beyond mere mortal strength and ability. If one thinks about a genocidal war and sees the images of mass graves one gets the message that more is at work here than mere human hatred. A human can hate God and all His creation but even that in itself requires a person to completely abandon all that his very breath rests on to exist. Some other source of strength must be at work, allowing the corrupted soul to continue in this state. God allows the human person to choose between Himself and evil, that which is a complete rejection of Him. To say that evil is simply a lack of God is not enough. True, evil often conquers in situations where good men fail to do the right thing; but there was more at work in the persecution and murder of six million Jews and the torture and murder of thousands of Christians in the Second World War than the absence of goodness. There was and there still is in this world a palpable evil in which death and destruction are the order of the day. Rape, incest, child abuse, murder, and many other horrors exist because evil exists. These are not just words but they are the basic reflection of a very terrible truth.

In *The Lord of the Rings* evil was one of the prominent features of the landscape. The orcs, the trolls, the wargs, and the ring wraiths were all sources of terrible evil. They were not figures that you would sit down in an analyst's chair and try to figure out. You wouldn't question whether they had a hard childhood or if they were simply being misunderstood by the society at large. One look at an orc and you just knew they were bad! It is nice to read a story where things are so simple and spelled out. It would be terrifying to meet an orc, but sometimes I wonder if life wouldn't be a bit easier if the servants of evil were so recognizable.

We cannot claim that there are a people or race that is evil in our world. To make such a blanket statement would be in itself a grave injustice and an evil act. We cannot point to an object and say that that is the source of all evil and if you destroy it we will finally be safe. If only it were that easy! In our society today we have many objects, tools and positions which can under the right circumstances be used to do the will of him who rejects God. In the spirit of rebellion and destruction, there are those who offer themselves as instruments of the devil and his cohorts. Evil exists and the devil rules his kingdom with a spirit as opposed to God and His goodness as one can get. But the devil cannot destroy the immortal soul. He does not have dominion over the universe as he would wish. His power to tempt and corrupt extends by the mystery of God to this Earth only. If a soul wishes to align himself to the powers of evil, then that choice can be made during the course of a lifetime and sealed at death. Once death occurs, then the die is cast, and the soul rejoices or suffers forever in the kingdom that it has chosen and as God's mercy and justice demand. Who would ever choose to serve a king who opposes God and who rules the kingdom of hell? Strangely enough, there are those who so lust after the small deceiving rings of power that they are blinded to the holy purpose of their existence, and they choose out of their own free will to serve that which will only cause them great suffering in the end.

The situation is clear on two points. Evil does exist. There is a devil and his unholy helpers whose sole aim is to cause as many souls as possible to reject God. There is a war going on; but it is not so much a battle of swords as it is a battle to reveal the truth and undeceive those who cannot see the light of Christ in this undeniably confusing world. The Shire is not so much at stake as are the souls of those who wish to live reborn on a "new Earth" and know Heaven as God would reveal it to those who love Him. It is a battle of wills over the souls of this Earth and it is far more fantastic, wonderful, and horrible than anything that Tolkien or anyone else could ever write about. It is a battle that has been going on since the dawn of time and will continue until Christ comes again in His glory to save the elect from the powers of darkness.

We all have a mission not unlike that of Sam and Frodo. We must respond to the call of our Hidden King to do His bidding and to represent His will in the land that we are given to work. We must face the challenges and terrors that befall us, and we must pray for every virtue and use every gift to endure the trials of our times. It is not easy to be a child of God, but it is well worth it. The petty temptations and lures of evil should make us shake our heads in wonder that anyone would choose their false worldly glitter to the reality of the hidden glory of God the Father, God the Son, and God the Holy Spirit. As Christ said, it is better to lose a hand or an eye than to risk the kingdom of God. Better to lose this Earthly body than lose our immortal souls.

How do we recognize these rings of power that assault us and our children? It may not be easy but it is far from impossible. There are seven capital sins which give us the first clue. Whenever we see these sins popping up before our eyes, then we might sit up and take notice that something bad is happening. First, we must identify these sins and then we must look at our world with a bright light and see the truth that stares us in the face. It is not easy because, frankly, sin is all around us. But once you see it, you can defend yourself and those you love more effectively by removing the source of temptation and spiritual harm. When Sam thought he had lost Frodo to the poison of Shelob, he considered his position despite his distress and decided that he had to go on, even though he could not imagine succeeding, and the price had already been more than he was willing to pay. It is with that spirit that no price is too high, and that only death will stop us from doing His glorious will upon this Earth, that we must face the perils which attack us every day.

It is only in the light of day that the orcs seem so terrible. In the dark, we can be deceived into thinking that a foe is really a friend. Although, we usually have to push down an inner repugnance and a healthy desire to get away. Too often, we have been forced to sit in waiting rooms and stare at television sets, or enticed to look at magazines and read books which cause us trepidation but which we have forced ourselves to endure and perhaps even enjoy. In fact, we have forced ourselves so often and so well that now we hardly react to scenes of violence or episodes of indiscretion that would have stood our ancestors' hair up on end. The time to light our lamps and walk forward is at hand. Let us march onward and be not afraid, for the hand that guides us is mighty indeed.

Pride

" 'Pride and despair!' he cried. 'Didst thou think that the eyes of the White Tower were blind? Nay, I have seen more than thou knowest, Grey Fool. For thy hope is but ignorance... The West has failed. It is time for all to depart who would not be slaves.'"
(The Return of the King)

Pride is a good thing! It is pride that gets us to mow the lawn so that our neighbors do not think the worst of us. It is pride in our children that prompts special rewards for good grades and excellent behavior. It is pride that allows us to keep our heads high even when we have a minor setback and have to face our limitations. Pride can be a good thing. At the right time and in the right amount, pride is a gift from God to help us remember that we are His, and we should not become like the animals. We are human beings and that is saying a lot.

The reverse side of pride as a detrimental force in our lives is rather simple. Whenever pride blocks our view of God, we are making a mistake. If we missed going to church because our pride dictated the need to mow the lawn so we would not be embarrassed, then pride sinks into a form of slavery. It no longer reminds us of a truth but deceives us into putting ourselves or our ideas before God.

Pride was Denethor's greatest weakness. He would not allow himself to be demoted to the honest position as Steward of Gondor when he had been living like the king. He would not believe that anyone knew better than himself, even though his source for information, the palantir, was deceitful. He would not accept good counsel even from his son, who was far more insightful than himself. His whole life was dedicated to upholding himself as the greatest person in the kingdom. He loved Boromir only in so far as Boromir was a continuing reflection of his own imagined greatness. Faramir refused to fit into his father's mold, and for that he was rejected. Even his death was a mere reflection of his life-long rejection of the greater mystery of his purpose. He was supposed to be and do things according to the will of One who was greater: and that meant that at times he had to put his own desires and plans on hold or ignore them or even sacrifice them so as to fulfill his role as true steward. But he would not. He wanted to be the king. He wanted to have his son offer him the power of the magic ring. He wanted to live and die by his own rules. Nothing was as important to Denethor as Denethor. He was his own God.

We think to ourselves, "Well, I am not like that! I go to church and I go to work and I obey my boss and I work hard and I even do what my spouse and kids want. Why, I am a virtual slave to everyone. I have no pride issues." It is interesting how pride can sneak in, and we hardly even notice it. Have you ever found yourself working at something till you are almost in a frenzy because it has to be perfect? And you aren't quite sure why it has to be perfect, but you feel it just has to be exactly so? When we offer an act or product to God, it is true we work really hard to do it well—but frenzy? What happens when we feel frenzied? We are being pushed so hard that there is some disorder taking place in our system.

I suspect that part of the reason we have crazy drivers and wild action-packed lives is not because we are called by the good God to live this way but rather because we feel we must. We are in a constant state of frenzy. Perhaps it is personal pride that drives our souped-up engines. We need coffee and soda just to keep going because life just isn't full enough. We hear, read, and learn through school and media that we are supposed to be super people. We need to know just about everything. We need to be able to cook those scrumptious recipes in the magazines and to decorate our houses like a designer and fix the plumbing like those guys on T.V. . Our kids need to play sports well, play at least one or two musical instruments, pass all sorts of tests, and become mature enough to handle our frequent absences. Everyone in our society is expected to be rather amazing. Grandparents not only help their kids and raise grandkids but do everything else besides, including going on trips so that they can see and learn new things. Life is so full and action-packed, is it any surprise we are so exhausted all the time? How is it that, though we are involved in so many good things and we are working so hard and trying our absolute best, we seem to be feeling empty and out of sorts, and the thought of God seems rather distant and Heaven seems almost ridiculous? Who wants more of this? It is already too much!

What is driving us? Who is driving us? The good Lord promises us that His burden is light. When we feel out of sorts and exhausted, there is a good reason. God our Father has built into our systems an overload sensation, but we often refuse to recognize it. We do more and want more, and we insist that all this stuff and action is necessary for our continued existence. But why are we afraid of failing? Are we afraid that God wants our sons to play baseball and they won't be able to stand before the throne of the Almighty without proving their ability to pitch a good curve ball? Or that God wants our kids to have sixteen good friends? Or that we must be thought of as the most helpful member on the school board? Or that our neighbors must not turn their heads aside in pain when they pass our house because the porch sags a bit?

Why are so many people in debt up to their ears? Because God doesn't want us to miss out on anything? Because God expects us as parents to give our kids the toys they want? Whom are we pleasing? Who is our God? Perhaps God has little to do with why we rush around or why we are maxing out our credit cards or why our houses are so big and our cars so new and on and on and on. We are tempted into thinking that we need stuff and we need to be doing things and we need to pass all this need onto our kids. But really, what does the Good Lord tell us is really important? What are the two greatest commandments? To love the Lord your God with all your heart and with all your soul and with your entire mind. Good heavens! One could be as poor as a country mouse with little to do but reflect on the beauty of the Lord's wonders and one could do as He really wants, quite adequately and even beautifully. The second command is to love others as you would like to be loved. How much rushing around is done so that we seem like good people and how much is because we simply love someone? Could we stay home and listen to our boy retell us his latest story or actually draw a picture with our daughter or call our neighbor for a chat or simply take time for quiet prayer? Do we need to rush about to love those God has placed at our side? The almighty Creator of Heaven and Earth knew what He was doing when He made us brothers and sisters. It is here at home that He expects us to practice the virtues, to offer love, and to sacrifice our wills. Here at home is where He works with us. Where is home and why do we need to leave it so much? Rush! Rush! Rush! Who is our God? To whom are we listening? Whom are we obeying? Good things are only truly good when they are in the service of the Lord. Pride is a good servant but an evil master.

Covetousness

" *'Down, snake!' he said suddenly in a terrible voice. 'Down on your belly! How long is it since Saruman bought you? What was the promised price? When all the men were dead, you were to pick your share of the treasure, and take the woman you desire?'"* (The Two Towers)

To covet is to wish for enviously. We covet all the time. It is Americans' normal pastime. Have you ever watched television? Advertisements are based on the human experience of covetousness. If we weren't tempted to covet, we wouldn't keep the stores so busy. This could also come under the heading of greed. We want more than we need. We want what others have. We want so much that we think of our wants as needs. We justify this sin as proper to our situation in life. In America everyone else has this or that or the other thing, and it hardly seems fair that we have been deprived of what everyone else has. We somehow deserve all this stuff, and we are being deprived if we don't have what others have. Greed and covetousness are probably the most excused sins in the world.

Let us take a good look at Saruman, the biggest self-deceiver in *The Lord of the Rings*, and his sidekick, Wormtongue. These characters have something in common: they both want what is not rightfully theirs. Saruman wants the Ring of Power so he can orientate the world to his own desires and fulfill his fantasies of becoming something great in the universe. He is not content with the power he has as the white wizard, he wants more. He creates a cruel and evil army to do his bidding to take by force what he cannot naturally have. Wormtongue is also a man who is not content with life as it unfolds naturally. He has a position high in the kingdom of Rohan, but he changes from trusted friend and servant to sly deceiving spy, so as to align himself with the rising power of Saruman. Look at how things really are. Both of these men have good jobs and great futures. They are in positions of trust and respect. They can do more and become more but always within a certain natural sphere. Life is good but just not good enough for their appetites. They do not consider right and a wrong and that they have been created for a noble purpose. That thought never seems to come into their heads. They have no thought of anything greater than themselves.

Gandalf was faced with an even more overwhelming argument when he is offered a choice between certain death or a life of power if he would simply align himself with the rising evil power of Saruman and Sauron. But he would not abjure his faith. He did not threaten Saruman with the power and anger of an even greater force; no, he simply stayed faithful. He had a strong desire to stay within his natural sphere. He did not want to tread the waters of powers beyond his capabilities. He knew his limits and he accepted them in the spirit of true humility: which is not only to know who you are but also rejoice in the fulfillment of that role.

So what happens to Saruman because of his greed and covetousness? The only thing that could happen to him. His sin becomes his undoing. What is sin? Sin is the rejection of God's will for us. To insist on doing, being, or having that which is not for us is to put ourselves in the place of God and suggest that we can do things better than He can. For example, if God has made you a man but you think you'd really rather be a robot, and you insist on having wires and tubes placed throughout your body, there is a very real chance that you will destroy yourself in the alteration process. That is not to say that a farmer can't become a merchant or a king can't become a simple servant. Those are roles and the Lord may call us to drastically change our roles in life several times. He has plans for us, and rejecting those plans may cost us more than we realize. Consider St. Francis of Assisi. He was a rich man's son who grew in holiness and abandoned the riches of the world to embrace the life God was offering as a mendicant friar (brother). He never strove for anything of greatness. He never even accepted the role as priest because he felt that God called him to utter poverty and simplicity. His choice was the reverse of most of our culture. Why was his role change admirable and others not? Because his did not involve the sin of covetousness and greed. When we covet, we are asking for what is not ours to have: that which rightfully belongs to another. It is not a sin to ask for food to feed your child, but it could be a sin to insist on always having the very best.

Covetousness is a very personal thing. We may covet what someone else is eating for dinner at a restaurant or covet the clothes on someone else's body. We may even covet another person's body! Magazines which lie around waiting rooms and offices often suggest that if only we have the thin muscular look of so-and-so, we would know a happiness that we have never yet experienced. The modeling industry plays upon our weakness towards covetousness. They hope we will want to look like someone else so we will buy their products and do whatever we desperately can to become what we are not.

We are not only encouraged to covet in this society: we are forced into the role of a coveter in all sort of "normal" conversations. "Oh, wouldn't you like to have that? It would be great to be that thin, healthy, strong, rich….." Rarely does a person say, "I am happy the way God made me, and my challenge is simply to love Him more." The greatest transformation that can happen to us is one that we cannot arrange or force. It is the transformation from sinner to saint. If we take a good look at Blessed Mother Teresa of Calcutta, we realize that she was exactly what God wanted her to be, and that she was beautiful beyond words.

And so it would have been with Saruman and Wormtongue. Some of the saddest moments in the trilogy are when the possibility of conversion is offered to them, and they each reject it. Imagine what could have been! They could have decided they were wrong and they could have repented. They could have changed so dramatically that they would have been figures of blessing instead of curses. Think of Scrooge in the story *A Christmas Carol.*

Because of his conversion he became a more beloved figure than one could have imagined possible.

And so it is with us. When we sit at table and eat more than we need, when we spend our more than adequate salary and end up in debt, when we dress to impress, and when we use more than our fair share of the world's resources, we are tending toward covetousness. We are breaking faith with the God who created us. It is not just a bad idea to be greedy and it is not just harmful to our self-esteem to be covetous, but it does injury to the whole world, and most importantly, it offends the Creator of the Universe, and that is not a good thing. This is a common sin, but that does not make it any less grievous.

Are we given the same option of conversion as Saruman and Wormtongue? Actually, as long as we are breathing we are being given the option of conversion. In a story, the point of conversion is usually seen at a climactic moment, and the choice is made "forever," so to speak. It is a very wonderful thing that we are not characters in a book. Our conversion can come anytime, and it may not be sudden or swift. In fact, those who are striving to be holy say it is a lifelong work. Every day we are offered choices between sin and holiness, and every day we must reaffirm the decisions we want to make. Sometimes we haven't thought too deeply about the matter and one day we will spend little on ourselves in a spirit of charity and humility and then the next day we are swept away on a spending spree. The problem with this uncertain direction is that once again we are putting ourselves in the place of God. I will try to be holy when I feel like it. I will sacrifice only up to a certain point. I will love you until I get uncomfortable. But that is hardly what the Redeemer asks of those who follow Him. Ask a saint, any saint, and you will get the same answer. God is surprising and He asks us to offer to Him the very things we don't want to give up, because there lays the greatest temptation. It seems the good Lord is not after our stuff as much as He is after our wills. He wants us to acknowledge Him as Lord of the Universe and to do His will even to the point of giving in on the little things of life.

It is one thing to give up "things" but another to give up time and space. Sometimes our covetousness can take the form of wishing we had someone else's job or position so we could do what we want. We are faced with the desire to want what is not ours or to sacrifice our desires. It becomes very hard not to want what looks so good from the outside. The road is narrow. Many people want to reject the path of letting go and being molded by God's loving hands. But only when we give up our selfish ways and our preoccupation with having more or better, only then can we possibly make room for God in our lives. The more stuff, the more wants, the more needs, the less emphasis we place on loving God. We turn God into a giving machine, but we do not love Him. Our love is only as deep as the fulfillment of our demands.

Saruman did not meet a good end. Wormtongue did not fare any better. It was tragic to see their corruption. But that is not the most important thing that we have to keep in mind. We are not characters in a book. For us living, breathing mortals with souls, we have to remember that we will live forever whether we like it or not. God created us, and He did not provide an off switch for our supernatural existence. Even when our human bodies cease to function, we will still live on; but where we will live will be determined by the perfect justice of God. God's mercy extends throughout this time on Earth. Our opportunity to embrace His mercy ends at our death. When the time of judgment comes, we will be faced with His truth; and there will be no clouding of the issues by our feeble explanation of how we always felt strong needs to have so many things. We will be faced with Him and the truth: whether we loved Him with our whole heart, our whole soul, and our whole mind.

It would be terrifying to die if we were not constantly being offered His grace in the virtues and gifts of the Holy Spirit. Hope exists for a reason. God created hope for He knew we would need it. It is through the virtue of hope that we face each day and try as hard as we can to become less greedy and less covetous and to grow in holiness.

Lust

> *" 'Too long have you watched her under your eyelids and haunted her steps.' " (The Two Towers)*

Lasciviousness refers to an unbridled desire. If one has watched television and gone to movies, it is pretty nearly impossible that you haven't been introduced to the evils of lust. Lust exists and is a dark secret in many a bosom. In fact it is probably the cause of more profound personal grief than all the other capital sins put together.

Wormtongue is an image of a lustful figure. In a strange sort of way so is Gollum. He seems to be so corrupt a figure that anything seems possible with him, and our mind fears to tread the lustful line, for we know it would lead to an evil end. Lust is a form of physical corruption. It is like greed in that we go beyond healthy limits, and we demand that which is not ours. But it is also a basic corruption that so alters everything it touches that the one in lust and the object of one's lust are both dehumanized.

In the Bible there is a very memorable scene when Abraham is warned that Sodom and Gomorrah are going to be destroyed and he begs for the lives of his kinsmen, reasoning that if there be just fifty good men then the whole city should be spared. The Lord in his mercy accepts this benevolent logic and even allows the number to be whittled down to ten. If there be just ten good men in the sight of God, he will spare the whole city. But otherwise the city will be destroyed. One wonders: if the Lord God is so kind as to be willing to change His mind and save the city for the sake of a few men, what on Earth could have induced such a great wrath that He would want to kill them all in the first place? If you read Genesis 18-19 you get a very clear picture of the events of the day. The Angel of the Lord had traveled to Sodom to clarify the matter of just how corrupt were the people and He was set upon while in Lot's house. Lot was the nephew of Abraham and was himself a just man with a clean heart. In other words, he did not live as the others in the city. This was a place of idolatry, where lust ruled the passions of the men to such an extent that they had no decency or mercy. The men of the town set upon Lot's house demanding that the Lord and His companions—whom they took for common travelers—be offered to them to satisfy their lustful appetites.

Lot did his best to fend them off, even to the point of offering his own two daughters, but they would have none of that. The men of the town wanted men to abuse. It is a rather terrifying scene and the heart is greatly troubled at the whole episode. Of course the Lord arranges matters so that they cannot break in; and when the morning comes, Lot is offered his salvation and that of his daughters if he will but flee to the mountain, for the city and the area round-about are to be destroyed. Not ten, not even five good men were found. Poor Lot, what became of his ten good men? Did he think his daughters' fiancés were just men? Did he hope that some neighbors would be found with clean hearts? Obviously he did not even see the magnitude of the evil which surrounded himself, his daughters, and his wife. Even his wife did not survive the adventure, for she was turned into a pillar of salt for disobeying the Lord when she looked back towards the destruction that would have been theirs but for the mercy of the good God. Disobedience can have a very high price.

There are several points here to think about. First, we might dismiss this whole story, saying that we are far too sophisticated to take it seriously. Why, it is all a metaphor for good and evil and, as everyone knows, we should be kind to travelers, so those towns got what they deserved by the simple fact that they weren't nice and they made God angry. We don't do that, because we are nice to everyone, and we don't do anything to upset Our Lord. No fire and brimstone here!

Tolkien wrote a story and it was a work of pure fiction. The Bible, on the other hand, is not just a good read. It is infinitely more. The Bible is the word of God and His truth is revealed through His word. Sodom and Gomorrah tell us more than we need to be "good". These two chapters light up a brilliant path for us to see. It is a path that leads to certain destruction and involves the sin of lust. The men of that town wanted to have relations with other men and this was wrong in the sight of God. There are other instances in the Bible where relations between men and men or women and women are condemned as an abomination. It is not socially acceptable to tell someone in our culture that what they do in the privacy of their home is within the domain of right and wrong. Yet, we do have laws against child abuse, rape, drug trafficking and a host of other offenses which are often done within the confines of a private home. So the fact that something is done privately does not give it a mantle of justice. And it was not simply the violence with which the Lord Himself was assaulted verbally and threatened; it was the whole corrupt history of the town which had called the Lord forth in the first place.

The Bible does not list the names and family groups of Sodom and Gomorrah, though surely they were known at the time and it is not often that names are not given. There is a great deal of space taken up in the Bible with genealogies. Yet, in these chapters the only persons named are the few just. We cannot account for the personal identity of the wicked that were destroyed. Now why is that? There is the possibility that the Lord wanted to condemn the sin clearly and not identify the sin with particular people. And so it is today: the church will condemn sin without forever condemning particular individuals because as long as breath is left in the body there is a chance for redemption and the sin may be repented.

The question arises in our modern minds, "What is so wrong with this particular sin?" We have a tendency to think that God has changed His mind about sin and that things wrong in the past may not be so today. Things do change and there is room for confusion; but sin is a corruption of our relationship with God. When we are in a state of sin, we are no longer free to fulfill the role that God has ordained for us. We are in some ways turning aside from His will to our own and choosing a deadly path that will lead us not towards the Heaven of union with our greatest good but towards a broken and separate agony which only those who are isolated from God forever can truly understand. In this particular case, corruption in men as well as in women is a situation where, though there may be a deep craving for the physical union with someone of the same gender, it is forbidden by God. In the case of Adam and Eve, if you remember, Eve broke her relationship with God simply by eating a piece of fruit. All fruit was not forbidden, just the fruit of one particular tree, the tree of knowledge of good and evil. One can see where Eve may have gotten a little confused as she pondered the apparent good of eating a delicious fruit which would bring her great physical pleasure as well as knowledge, but there was one simple thing she failed to heed: the word of God. She simply reasoned the issue out herself and found that the apple was good for her, and she even led her husband into the same sin by offering the fruit to him using her own self-deceiving arguments as reasoning. Thus he did not think of God's will, and he too sinned.

The fact of the matter is that God's word is enough. If the Lord God decided to tell us all on Earth this day that we should never ever kill another mosquito, we would be very wise to obey. We do not need to argue with God or try to reinterpret His thoughts. Our job is to obey because we are His children, and He loves us as a merciful Father. The nice thing is that most of the time we can reason out the whys and what-ifs of God's laws. For the most part they make a great deal of sense. Sin cannot be truly reasonable because God is our greatest good. Even if we were to die a terrible death, it would be better to die with no sin than to choose to sin and break our relationship with God. There are numerous events in the Bible narrating particular individuals' faithfulness even though it meant certain death. There are thousands and thousands of martyrs who suffered and died so as to preserve their relationship with God above all things. God does understand more than we know, and He has shown greater mercy than we deserve; but that does not justify our choosing personal sin, no matter how private it may be.

Lust is a common sin. It is very common for two people to live together or for a man or woman to have multiple partners. Christ is pure, and He wants us to be pure whether we are married in faithfulness or single and chaste. Lust is an act of putting ourselves before God. We decide we know what is best for ourselves and those we hold in our power. It rarely seems to occur to us these days that we will live forever and this life is our proving ground. This is our time to choose and it is not our "right" to choose, it is our God-given gift to choose. We choose whether we will offer everything in this temporary world to God in order to gain the Eternal Kingdom. The Lord Jesus Christ never once offered us perfect happiness here on Earth. On the contrary, he offered us a cross.

Every time a person gives in to the sin of lust, a momentary pleasure is chosen over the everlasting happiness of eternal life with God. Here and now seems so real, but it only lasts for a short time. Turn your mind to Sam and Frodo. Sam never once acted immodestly towards Frodo though he was very loving in every healthy sense of the word. He never crossed the bounds between love and lust. Not in the whole book is there any scene in which Tolkien makes a person blush with shame or skip the pages so that children will not be scandalized. Tolkien did not justify sin. He made sin apparent and ugly.

We are forced in many instances in this society to consider the feelings of a sinner and thus take pity on his or her needs and wants. But we forget, we are commanded by God to love Him with all our heart, with all our minds and with all our soul. We can never love another enough to excuse forgetting this first command. The first is first and it must be followed first. It costs us comfort and personal ambition and even pleasure and happiness at times. To do God's will and to abandon our lusts is to do a very hard thing. It means breaking off relationships and hurting feelings. It means telling the truth to family members who won't always understand and who might not like us so well. It means living a more lonely life on Earth with fewer personal comforts. It means going against the current of common reasoning. The path away from evil is similar to the road to Mordor. There are dangers all around. We are not certain of our salvation. But we offer our very lives, and we carry on past fatigue, past endurance, past hope into the supernatural world of God's grace. We can throw away the ring of lust and put it to its rightful end in the burning furnace of Mount Doom. We can avert our eyes to television shows that tempt us, or even turn the television off when it is offensive. It might end up being off most of the time, but life does go on. We can let those magazines drop from our fingers when they tempt our eyes towards things that we cannot have and would be better off not wishing for. We can choose different places for entertainment than those that involve vice and sin. In time, we can offer to God hearts purified from all evil, and He will find us pleasing in His sight and then our joy will be complete. Sam might well have pondered the stars as he guarded his friend at night. The stars will all blow out one day, but the soul of a human being will never cease to be. We were made to live forever.

Anger

"Thieves! Fire! Murder! Such a thing had not happened since first he came to the Mountain! His rage passes description – the sort of rage that is only seen when rich folk that have more than they can enjoy suddenly lose something that they have long had but have never before used or wanted." (The Hobbit)

Anger refers to an intense emotional state triggered by some displeasure. Once again we have a situation where we are asked to consider the difference between justice and sin. There are both justified anger and sinful anger, but there is a terrific difference between them. Aragorn got angry when he learned that Pippin and Merry are captured by the orc raiders. Pippin and Merry are angry when Boromir is killed. Treebeard is angry when he learns what Saruman has done to his forest and his friends. There are many instances of justified anger. Terrible things happen in life, and they make us mad. We feel our blood boil at the murder of an innocent child or the horror of merciless genocide or the calculating cruelty of a robbery. We find ourselves becoming very hot. There is a good reason for this. Sometimes we tend to be a little too accepting of sin, for an object at rest tends to want to remain at rest, and, too often, unless we get upset, we would rather just not bother ourselves with a given situation, especially if it involves a messy emotional scene.

It is our ability to empathize, and thus to feel the pain of another, that causes us to imagine what we would feel like in the horror of any given suffering. When we imagine we suffer, we tend to *really* suffer, and that makes us mad. We don't want to suffer, and we don't want others to suffer. We don't even like to know of animals suffering. It is a built-in defense and more than that. Once again the good Lord has graced us with an ability to be greater than a machine and greater than any animal or plant. We have the unique ability to feel each other's pain and want to do something to stop the suffering of ourselves and others.

Anger can be very useful in that it can lift us out of an accepting stupor and make us jump up, ready to act. But why is it considered one of the capital sins? For the same reason that every sin is a sin. The disordered use of an emotional response can lead us to act contrary to God's will. Disorder is the key word. Instead of getting mad at a grave injustice we get mad because our coffee is not hot. Or instead of using our anger to solve an injustice, we decide to burn down a building. Either we overreact to something that is simply not that serious and does not warrant our furious indignation, or we react to sin with another sin. Sin cannot justify sin. Again it comes down to the basic principle that our life experience on this Earth is temporary. We cannot justify breaking our relationship with God so that we can have peace here on Earth. We cannot kill all the murderers because it seems to make sense to our minds. We cannot kill all the people who do evil things, because God has ordained that this time on Earth is a time of mercy, and we all hold this time as a chance of redemption. No one has the right to take God's time of mercy away from another, no matter how grave the sin may be. We are simply never allowed to stand in the place of the Lord God. We may suffer agony of heart and mind every day, reliving the horror that was inflicted on the innocent by the evil actions of a sinful mind, but that does not hand us the authority of God. We have the right to defend ourselves, and in an act of defense someone might die; but that is not the same as premeditated murder.

War is one of those horrible human situations where we expand the notion of protection; for the danger might not be limited to a single human threat but may involve the massive effort of a nation. Self-preservation is allowed, but vengeful murder is not. Only the Lord God can take a life. In fact, if you believe the words and actions of Jesus, then one would be hard pressed to give a good case for the horror of war. It is true though that the Church Herself has recognized its necessity in the face of aggressive, destructive evil such as with the case of Nazi Germany in the Second World War. The Church has always counseled peace first and throughout even the most terrible situations as the best way of resolving differences; but the fact remains that evil exists and there is no possible way to make peace with an evil agenda. Those involved may change their thoughts and plans, and reconciliation can be possible with former enemies, as we have seen time and again; but good can never shake hands with evil. Gandalf simply cannot reason with Saruman. And no one in Middle-earth would have survived if Sauron was allowed to continue on his way.

Anger as well as war are situations where the human soul must be directed by a higher force than mere emotionality. The framework of reason used within the precepts taught by the word of God and through the genius of the Magisterium are our guides here on Earth. God does not abandon us to figure everything out on our own. He knows how easily shaken and confused we can become, so He lives still in the Church, which nurtures and guides us as a loving parent. On the personal level we have priests and pastors who can be consulted for individual situations to help enlighten us as to the direction we should take when we are feeling upset by a circumstance or event. We are blessed with the guidance of the encyclicals and councils which the popes and magisterium have offered to humanity as thoughtful, Holy Spirit-induced reflections to help us along our way as a people of God.

Gandalf understood very well these dual principles of thought filled mercy and guidance. He understood it better than poor, frustrated and distracted Sam. Sam wanted to kill Gollum on more than one occasion, and he had great reasons for accusing Gollum of evil intentions; for the fact was that Gollum did have evil intentions. Gollum had a very disordered heart and mind. Yet even so, redemption was still possible. As we learned, he had a part to play that was ordained from on high. Gandalf did not run from his position as counselor when faced with the situation by telling Frodo what he wanted to hear when he was infuriated and disgusted by Gollum's sneaking presence. He did not merely reflect Frodo's feelings back at him. He was willing to risk the possibility that Frodo, and Sam by extension, would not understand and would simply do whatever they wanted and thus grow angry at Gandalf for not supporting them. Gandalf knew that to counsel according to the wisdom of God is to try to explain things that may seem foolish and extraordinary to those who cannot yet see the greater truth.

If it were possible, it would be nice to write a list of all the ways that anger could be good and healthy, and then all the ways that anger crosses the line and leads towards sin. But that is simply not possible. Life is much too complicated, and the human heart much too involved, for such a simplistic approach. As always, we must rely on a healthy prayer life, exercise of the virtues, and the guidance of those who are wiser than ourselves. In all humility, it is possible to experience anger and yet not be enslaved by it. For the Lord Himself has grown angry many times. Anger is a natural, healthy response to evil. Let us prayerfully do all that we can so that we never do evil in His sight, becoming the object of His mighty wrath.

Gluttony

"This is worse than Mordor!" said Sam. "Much worse in a way. It comes home to you as they say; because it is home, and you remember it before it was all ruined."

"Yes, this is Mordor," said Frodo. "Just one of its works. Saruman was doing its work all the time, even when he was working for himself. And the same with those that Saruman tricked, like Lotho."

Merry looked around in dismay and disgust. "Let's get out!" he said. "If I had known all the mischief he had caused, I should have stuffed my pouch down Saruman's throat."

"No doubt, no doubt! But you did not, and so I am able to welcome you home." There standing at the door was Saruman himself, looking well-fed and well-pleased;..." (The Return of the King)

Gluttony means excessive indulgence. This is one of those sins that the cartoons do a great job of making fun of, yet we are encouraged to engage in this sin all the time. The Lord God created things in such a way that there was a wonderful balance and symmetry in the world. Though sin has corrupted much, there is still a natural force of balance which helps to guide us and keep our actions in check. But we humans are so smart, we like to go around cheating the scales so to speak, so that we can do what we want and not have the negative consequences of our actions.

In the book, *The Lord of The Rings*, Denethor is definitely a man out of balance, yet the movie made a special scene which highlighted this point very well. After Denethor has sent Faramir away on a useless and destructive mission, Denethor is seen eating at table while he orders Pippin to sing, though the only songs the poor Hobbit knows are really not appropriate to the situation. Still, the father ignores his son's peril and goes on eating as if he has nothing better to do. It is a terrible and repulsive scene. Yet, sometimes I wonder if the Lord our God has to endure much the same scene every day with us mortals here on Earth. There are poor families, mothers who cannot feed their babies, and fathers offering all they have to care for their little ones, yet they cannot feed, clothe or properly care for themselves much less their children. The heartless would simply condemn those who can't make do for daring to think that they are worthy to experience the joy of parenthood and that if they were smart they'd just not have kids. It makes us mighty uncomfortable to keep the poor in mind as we drink our diet sodas, eat our fat-free chips, wolf down our cholesterol-free eggs, and basically indulge in overeating foods that are made to taste similar to real food but do not have any of the balancing effects which would normally keep us from eating more than our fair share. It takes energy and resources to make such food. It takes research, time, and money to develop new ways to indulge our appetites without feeling the effects. How must the Lord feel as He watches us chow down and complain because we are getting fat while He experiences the suffering of our innocent brothers and sisters who do not have enough to live?

Granted, our personal gluttony may not be the source of the world's poverty: but the sin is still there. Whenever we eat more than we need, and partake of the lion's share of the world's resources, we are out of balance with God's natural plan, and it isn't really all that funny. The cartoons make us laugh as a silly character gobbles up everything on the table, but gluttony is a serious sin. We are encouraged to the point that we have become so twisted in our thinking that we feel guilty if we don't give our kids great-tasting fat free snacks and such a wide variety of foods that our children are inundated with food they do not feel comfortable with because nothing is ever familiar. We actually feel guilty if we don't indulge our families with desserts, snacks, and treats of all varieties and shapes all the time. One wonders how the human race survived up until the time the recipe-of-the-month club came along in our favorite home-loving magazines! Go ahead, spend a fortune on all sorts of ingredients and take hours of time to prepare the best low-calorie, fat-free, zero-cholesterol, practically nonexistent food you can. Forget that there are in reality many people who are scraping their bowls for the last bite of rice, and they are still hungry. Their bodies are craving that fat we are trying desperately to avoid.

The fact of the matter is that personal sin affects the world. When we eat more than is good for us and ignore the very real suffering of the poor, we swing out of God's natural balance. It tends to make our gluttony our god, and thus all sorts of poor systems and some downright evil systems rule the food industry. We forget our role as stewards of the Earth and consider ourselves kings to be pleased at any cost. We are no longer servants of the Most High but we put His creation at our feet and demand the unreasonable and the impossible. We want more than is fair, and we don't want to feel guilty. We want to eat more than is healthy, and we don't want to get sick. We want to have great tasting food, cheap and available, while we do not want to consider the long-range implications of our actions.

So how do we escape such a cycle? The first issue is to realize that we do have a part to play in the world and that any act, no matter how small, does make a difference. We may not change the world but we can take a step by simply eating to live, not living to eat. Our Lord ate at social gatherings, but one feels pretty confident that He didn't stuff Himself. Almost every saint you read about will reaffirm that the path to holiness involves a level of self-discipline and sacrifice. Our human natures are such that we cannot indulge ourselves for any length of time without peril to our soul. We must be ever vigilant. Do not look to a particular person to lead you on to the diet of holiness. It just does not work that way. If diets were holy we would be a nation of saints. But actually diets can be just another form of gluttony. Saint Francis made the rule that his followers were to simply to eat what was set before them without complaint. When we insist on eating only a certain kind of food because we are on a special diet, we often cross the line into selfishness once again. We have got to have what we want. This is not necessarily need-based, but more simply a reflection of a society which has put diets on the level of mini-gods who are to be obeyed at all costs while the mood lasts. But diets are rarely successful in alleviating the problem of overeating for one simple reason. They don't address the problem. Sin is the problem. Self-indulgence is the problem. Brokenness with God is the problem.

How do we deal with any sin? Prayer and grace. We ask for God to help us, and we try our hardest to conform our will to His. We turn from gluttony to love of God and love for our brothers and sisters. We turn away from irresponsible buying habits to slowly but surely taking responsibility for the resources we consume. We take our role as stewards of our Earth seriously. Once again comfort is not the issue. Salvation is the issue. No one can be perfect but most of us have plenty of room for improvement. It is a matter of the heart and the soul as well as the mind. Being gluttonous is not reasonable any more than it is morally justifiable. The truly necessary thing for the human soul is that we love God with all our hearts, all our minds, and all our strength. This will bring us the joy and pleasure which we long for. That is within the reach of the rich as well as the poorest of the poor. Man cannot live by bread alone.

Envy

"Even were his claim proved to me, still he comes but of the line of Isildur. I will not bow to such a one,..."

"What then would you have," said Gandalf, "if your will could have its way?"

"I would have things as they were in all the days of my life," answered Denethor,.... "But if doom denies this to me, then I will have naught: neither life diminished, nor love halved, nor honor abated." (The Return of the King)

"Envy is a painful and resentful awareness of an advantage enjoyed by another and a desire to possess the same advantage." (*Merriam Webster's Collegiate Dictionary*) Envy, taken to its final outcome, must end as Denethor's life did, in a fiery doom; for it is quite impossible to become another person or truly attain the qualities which cause us to feel envious in the first place. Each person is unique because that is how God wants us to be, and it is in our very unique nature that we will find our greatness. Envy is like covetousness in that we wish we had something that is not ours, but usually envy involves the wish to have qualities which the Lord in His wisdom chose to offer to another.

It can seem downright unfair that so-and-so has a photographic memory while we struggle to memorize our phone number. Yet, there is a good reason for this apparent inequity. I used to simply believe rather naively that all people were created equal because that is what we are taught to believe in school. But as I grew older and reality set in, I came face to face with the truth that we human beings are many things, but one thing we are not is equal.

Not on this Earth. We are all so different, with various gifts and weaknesses, that it is rather impossible to take an accurate stock of oneself much less each other. We are able to plainly see that in truth some people are highly gifted while others are not so. It would only be true to say that we are equal if one added the phrase, "in the eyes of God," because in truth we are all very small in comparison to the infinite qualities of God. It is highly ironic that our modern society has done so much to separate itself from the religious orientation of God, for our nation is built upon the one principle that must include God in order to be true: "We are created equal in the eyes of God."

In *The Lord of the Rings* we do not find this dual reality. In fact, we find the complete acceptance of the facts of individuality gleaming out of all sorts of unexpected places. Tom Bombadil is hardly a classifiable person, and he is certainly on a level that is beyond the full comprehension of most if not all the characters. Beorn is another character which defies a definitive place and value. We are simply left to accept these characters as being quite above the average. One has to admit they are special and that it is not in the power of a Hobbit to become like Tom or Beorn. It is not possible and it would do little good to envy the greatness of another. The gift in the story is that envy never really seems an issue. It is almost as if there are few who need to sully themselves with such sin. Greatness is admired and revered as a gift given from on High, and those who need help admit their humble station, looking no further for glory. In fact, it is one of the more endearing traits of the Shire that most of the inhabitants don't want to look to greater things but are quite content in the quiet simplicity of their own natural elements.

For us, in this world today, we could easily blame so many tempting entertainments for creating alluring situations where it seems that, if we did this or that, we too could become greater than we are. We watch movies and television and we see people who are funny, attractive, and rich besides. They seem like us in many ways, but they are also tantalizingly different. If only we had that furniture or dressed in such a way or talked in such witty, sarcastic ways, we too could be as they are. We could be full of the charm of a half hour sit-com or the hour drama. There are so many ways that such dream stuffs are sold to us under the illusion that we could become someone else. Basically the dual lie is that you are as good as anyone else, but we can help you change yourself completely.

If it weren't for the fact that such distractions do a great deal of harm to our souls, the whole situation would be funny. But since the harm is buried under mountains of materialistic goods and efforts to make ourselves funnier, prettier, smarter, stronger, and wealthier, it all seems good in the long run. There is only one universal problem. We are who God created us to be, and He has a plan that is far better than any magazine article, television commercial or imaginary character. He offers us a life beyond this life. He offers us Himself. But we have to be willing to forego all the tempting allurements of this world and concentrate on His will for us. And His will doesn't necessarily involve make-up and exercise equipment.

Some would say that we are an obsessed culture, having a very weak sense of our personal worth, and thus we are really hiding atrocious cases of low self-esteem. It certainly could be on individual bases at different times of our lives. But the money that is thrown into various get-rich, get-beautiful, get-smart schemes is staggering. We could probably end poverty in the world if we simply limited our expenses to simpler forms of health care and education and offered our excess to those more in need. Our need to be something great or to "be somebody" reflects not a weak ego but an ego out of place.

Every person that the Lord God creates is somebody. As a matter of fact, every person is somebody infinitely important. That is why it is wrong to abort a baby in the womb or to euthanatize a sick, handicapped or old person. Our level of development or condition does not define our humanity or our worth. We are worth something because God loves us, and He has decided we are worth something. He thinks we are worth enough to come to Earth and suffer to be as one of us in all things but sin. He thinks are worth dying a humiliating death for. He thinks we are worth rising to life again for. We can never do anything to add to the worth that God has given to us. If we feel the slightest gratitude to Him for His love and attention, then it would behoove us to do what He wants and not waste our time trying to chase after imaginary alter-egos.

We are not able to rearrange the world and make "all things right" according to our own will and sentiment. We are only able to be who God has sent us to be and do His will. If we do that, then there is hope that we may gain the kingdom of Heaven and meet our brothers and sisters in the perfect peace of God's glory. Then, and only then, will we be free of our desire to be "equal," for we will know ourselves for who we truly are.

No matter how hard we try, we will never acquire the qualities of that person whom we secretly envy. Our hope lies in the fact that we have not yet fulfilled the potential which God has set for us. The issue is to avoid being confused. Loud blaring commercials and glittery magazines seem to tell us that they can aid us in becoming who we were meant to be. There is illusion rather than truth in that empty promise. It is like the Ring of Power. It seemed to offer great personal strength, but the smart characters knew in their hearts that it was all a trick, an empty distraction which would lead not to fulfillment but to destruction.

How do we learn to lead lives of holiness and perfection? How do we become our best selves? We ask the good God who made us. He promised that He would answer us. But beware that even our own minds can deceive us and that it is wise to ask a wiser person than ourselves from time to time if we are on the right track. Humility is a good antidote to the outrages of an ego which knows no bounds. Envy is a sin. It is no friend to us or to our families. It has no place in a loving relationship. When faced with the ugly specter of personal envy, it is best to confess our faults and then do our utmost to root it out. Once it seems gone, we can never let our vigilance fail, for it is a fault that likes to rear its ugly head again and again. Our security and worth lie not in how much we are loved but in how much we can truly and with all our hearts learn to love others.

Sloth

" 'Those are the golden sessions,' writes Lewis, 'when our slippers are on, our feet spread out towards the blaze and our drinks at our elbows; when the whole world, and something beyond the world, opens itself to our minds as we talk;'" (J.R.R. Tolkien: A biography p.148)

Sloth is a kind of indolence where we have disinclination to action or labor. This seems too easy. Don't be lazy. We know what that means. It is something we are told from little tykes on up to old age. "Get up! Keep moving! Don't be a lay-about! Get off the couch! Get out of bed! Why the birds are up!!!!!" We can hear the bugle blare of demands from the second we arise in the morning. So that is what God wants from us, eh? He wants us to keep moving and never stop. He wants us to be lean, mean fighting machines!

Did you ever notice how Tolkien seemed to take a certain pleasure in making parts of his story move very, very slowly? It seems as if he were simply strolling along. He described everything. Even things you really didn't want to know about. He even had the infuriating habit of telling you the names of persons and places in different languages or from different times in history. Not time-efficient. But why? He obviously had a vivid imagination, and he could have kept the action going pretty near all the time had he wished to. But he did not wish to. He kept slowing things down for long spells and making the characters rest and thus we had to rest and look around so to speak. They pondered and we pondered. It was almost therapeutic. I wonder if that isn't part of the charm of his books: that you really do go on a journey. But the journey is not like some of our rushed vacations where we have limited time, and we have to hurry on to the next activity at every step. In *The Lord of the Rings* the reader is invited to experience, not only a world, but also a way of life that is very different from ours. The characters are mainly humble folk who are not looking for greatness but find that quite suddenly they are thrust into a fight that means the salvation of the world as they know it. But yet they are still themselves, and their world still is the ordinary place of fields, streams, woods and rocks. It is true that they are faced with physical dangers most of us will never have to know, but I wonder how very different our struggle really is. The difference may not be in the essentials so much as our perception of the value of who we are and what we are doing here on this Earth at this time. Amazingly, it is the twisted notion of sloth that most blurs our vision.

We are too busy. We are working or doing something all the time. Everything is so terribly important. Often we are doing more than one thing at a time. "Multi-tasking" it is called. So we live lives of rush and near panic because we have so much to do and so much we yet want to finish and so much that is tantalizing us that we may not get to it all before we die. Twenty-four hours is certainly not enough time to complete the average day. It feels kind of wild and wonderful at times to be so busy. We are alive and living to our capacity. Everything, from our calendar to the minutes of our day, is full to the max. Better yet, it seems that most of what we are doing is really great stuff. God will be pleased that I am taking such good care of the house, and the laundry is pretty decent, and I got all the bills paid, and my kids are doing pretty well at their respective sports. They all have play time and some music lesson or another. We go on vacation and visit the relatives. We eat good food, and I keep the meals interesting. The house needs painting, but that will wait a season because we are fixing up the basement this year. All this stuff keeps our minds and bodies in action. Life is good.

But is that all we are here for? The Hobbits who lived in the Shire would probably say, "Yes, but slow down." They would argue for the simple pleasant existence of people who do what is in their sphere of family and friends and that should be enough. But there are other forces at work in the world. There is evil and darkness of soul which likes to creep upon us unawares. Were we created to have a good life here on Earth? Is that what we were brought into being for? To live well? If one says no, one will be condemned as a crazy person, but if one says yes, one risks ignoring the very real words of Christ, who promised us contradiction and suffering on this Earth. Jesus does not want to make us suffer. He would hardly be the source of our salvation if that were the case. But the fact is that we are not called to rest in our Earthly pleasures. Yet, that does not mean we should be frenetically busy either.

Sloth is one of those vices that the enemy of God must have enjoyed playing with. He has so blinded our eyes to the notion of rest that he has made us think that unless we are very busy we are committing a sin. But the question to ask is; are we busy doing what God wants us to do or are we busy trying to find happiness and comfort? Is that bad? No, but what is better? Pleasing God or satiating ourselves? And how can we ever know what God wants if we never have any time for Him? Sunday worship is not enough. That is like a starvation diet of prayer. Jesus gave us a prayer in which He teaches us to ask for our daily bread. Why daily? Would it not be much more efficient to ask for our weekly bread or our monthly ration? But that is not how God or our minds and souls work. The Lord made us. He knows how we operate. He knows our hard wiring. If we don't have continual contact with something, we tend to forget it and replace it with something of greater attraction. Since prayer takes effort and is sometimes difficult, we tend to skip it and go on to other more pressing matters. But notice how Tolkien forced his characters, in the midst of their great struggles, to stop and wait. They were forced again and again to simply rest, look, listen and be still. It is at these times that the characters gain the strength of will to do the task which seems quite impossible yet is very necessary. They each have a task to do and no one else can take their place. Each character is forced to rely on all his personality and reserves of strength in order to respond to the grace which allows them to go beyond the possible into the realm of the supernatural.

We are conceived in our mothers' wombs so that we can lead effective lives which demonstrate our love of God. We might be sick in bed or dashing up a steep hill, but the call and the effectiveness of our lives could be very similar if we are doing with great love what God wills for us. We are called forth from nothing into being by a God who has a master plan, and He has certain tasks for each one of us that no one else can do as well. We are all equal in our worth because God has caused us all into being for a purpose. Our purpose may be to live but a short time but to love God very well during that time. We may be called to live long and lead others to His light. We may be called to do difficult yet glorious battle against the enemy who assaults the weak and innocent. We may be called to live lives of quiet justice and witness the love of a mother for her children and lead them to love God with all their souls. The issue is not how busy we look or how many things we are getting done or even how effective we are in the world's eyes but rather how much do we please the Lord who created us.

It is so hard to slow down that I remember feeling a bit lonely and out of sorts each time I unplugged from an activity which claimed an unwarranted amount of time and attention. The loss of being connected to the television world took months to get used to. Saying no to temptations is hard work! It sounds so simple to slow down, but it is not easy. Being quiet with God can arouse deep feelings. Suddenly we are alone with some uncomfortable thoughts and memories. No one really likes to remember past mistakes, much less repent them, but we all have a duty, not only to remember and to repent, but also to try to do some form of reparation. It is like going on a journey. One would make a list of all the things needed to make the journey successful, but the fact is that we should all be spending time preparing for the greatest journey of all. We will pass from this life into the next most certainly yet that realization seems to have slipped our busy brains. We figure we will get to it when we have time, when we are older or retired, when the kids are grown or we are finished with the project at hand. Yet it is a journey we are all sure to make and few of us have made any better preparations than to perhaps buy a plot of ground and pick out the funeral home. That may take our bodies into the ground, but will it take our souls to God? So what do we do? Well, this is where sloth is really a sin. We get up off our spiritual couches and we pray. We go to church. We listen to the homily with humility, and we offer ourselves to God. We need to sincerely repent our sins, and we gain from the sacraments the grace to move forward towards our ultimate goal. If we are committing the same sin over and over it really isn't okay. If we are losing our temper with our kids and spending more money than we have and keeping so busy that our spouses have forgotten who we are, then we have to consider a serious change.

The sin of sloth is a tricky one. We are a very slothful people when it comes to the spiritual life. It just does not seem as important as the physical world which confronts our senses each day. But the spiritual world is far more real and of greater consequence than we will know this side of the great divide. We need to rouse our spirits from slumber and work for the salvation of us all.

Chapter Five
Lead Us Not Into Temptation

"One Ring to rule them all, One Ring to find them, One Ring to bring them all and in the darkness bind them." (The Fellowship of the Ring)

"How art thou fallen from heaven, O Lucifer, who didst rise in the morning? How art thou fallen to the Earth that didst wound the nations?" (Is xiv 12)

"You are of your father the devil, and the desires of your father you will do. He was a murderer from the beginning, and he stood not in the truth; because truth is not in him. When he speaketh a lie, he speaketh of his own: for he is a liar, and the father thereof." (John viii 44)

The devil exists and the creation of certain evil trends in our society has been promoted through the unreasoning reason of his great lies. If you take a good thing and twist it a bit, you can sell it to a lot of people as still a good thing. Or if you mix a good thing with a bit of evil, you can still convince a fair number of people that the evil isn't so bad, and we need not be too worried. Thus evil gains a foothold, and our children see our example and swallow the good with the bad. They lose their sensitivity to the difference between good and evil, because we simply have forgotten to draw thick lines. We insist that there are exceptions and that we should not be unreasonable.

All the while the devil laughs because we are simply too busy to think things through and soon we take in great evil, simply because we are too tired to fight or even protest. Somewhere inside us, our exhausted soul stirs, and we feel some shame or guilt, but we don't want to deal with it, so we fall asleep, and the next morning we get busy again and the cycle repeats itself. The gap between us and God gets wider, and soon we have lost our hearing and our sight. It is a lamentable time when we no longer care that the face of God is far from us. It is tragic that we make a joke that when we die, we will need field glasses to even see the traces of Heaven. It is not really acceptable to leave ourselves in this situation. It is not all right to make a truce with the evil in our lives. It is not good to accept a ring of power into our homes even for a little while. We cannot call ourselves one of the faithful when we are not even trying to be faithful all the time. Everyone slips at times, but no one can accept a slip and call it comfortable.

There is a hell, and it will not be comfortable. Hell (Gehenna) is described by Jesus as a burning fire. We don't like that image so we tend to discount the thought by suggesting that Jesus was only speaking figuratively. He didn't really mean that we will burn in the fires of hell forever if we stray from the path of God and His merciful redemption. Or did He? Certainly, we know He was not known for joking around. We know He was warning us. It is strange how we are so ready to believe in the joys of Heaven but so reluctant to believe in the torments of hell. We are offered choices all the time, and we think that we were given these rights and freedoms by the Constitution or by our legal system when the fact is that our God is the one who has given us these things. We may not experience the natural consequences of our choices because this country is tolerant of evil. We tend as a nation to accept almost every form of behavior as simply different but not deviant. The choice is still ours by the very reality of our existence as children of God; but the just consequence of our choices may not be known until the time of judgment.

So, what are these evils and temptations in our society? They are the tools which, misused, can do us great harm. They are not necessarily evil in themselves, but they do us great harm by giving us the idea that because we have the power and freedom to use these things so we have the right to explore them to their depths and use whatever means necessary to achieve personal happiness, pleasure or security. It is once again a question of who is God in our lives. Sam was someone who may not have named God, but he knew to his inner core that he was the servant of his Master, and for him the Master's will still existed even when Frodo fell.

Is that true for us? Is God still God for us even when we have lost that which meant the most to us on this Earth? Then why do we cling to anything which may separate us from Him?

Computers and Television

"At first the globe was dark, black as jet, with the moonlight gleaming on its surface. Then there came a faint glow and stir in the heart of it, and it held his eyes, so that now he could not look away." (The Two Towers)

Computers and televisions are possible sources of evil though not necessarily evil in themselves. What they represent is somewhat like the ring of power. They offer us power to have what no human beings have ever before had. They can be useful but dangerous tools. How else did we get to see *The Lord of the Rings* in full color? The world has changed drastically in the last few years since television and computers have made their debut. One might even say that the human race has changed as a whole in response to this new technology. It is absolutely impossible to put all the pros and cons in a scale and say that the world was better before or better now. The only way we could accurately judge would be if we had the knowledge of God. But the actual merit of television or computers is not in question. What is in question is whether it can do us great harm.

The Palantir was one of the seven crystal globes created by the Noldor, the Elves, and given to the Lords of Anduie, men, by the Eldar. The palantir could show scenes that were far away in time or space or could be used for communication. It was a tool to be used by those who were strong enough to control it. Much the same could be said about television and computers. They are useful tools in the hands of the strong and self-disciplined but very dangerous in the hands of the weak or childish. Denethor was overcome by the power of the palantir even though he was a grown man in a position of authority. It is not the age, size or position of a person that makes him or her able to handle the dangerous tools of life. It is really the level of self-discipline that one acquires through a life of continuous struggle with the temptations which hound our very footsteps.

Television is dangerous in that it offers a host of sinful temptations from vivid scenes of impurity and graphic scenes of violence to a continuous line of covetous tidbits. If the Lord Himself said that the man who simply lusts in his heart has already committed a sin then what is happening in living rooms and bedrooms throughout our country where explicit fare is offered on a continuous basis?

The ironic thing about this situation is that practice in the art of watching television does not make you better but rather makes you weaker. A person's sensitivity to sin and scenes which should evoke horror is quietly worn away. It seems as if nothing special is happening as you sit in the chair taking in picture after picture of immodesty and aggression, physical as well as verbal, but the person who is receiving all these blows to their virtue is actually becoming weaker and more distant from the God of justice and purity. Could one honestly imagine the Lord God wanting to sit through the average television show and its accompanying commercials? When my family stopped watching television we had to cut ourselves off completely for a long period of time in order not to be tempted to just see this little thing or that. The transformation was hard and took some time. Strangely enough it was sort of lonely without the box on. But as time passed we found that the peace in the house was far greater than it had ever been. Also, I found I had a great deal more time to do the things I had never been able to get to, like taking a walk with the family every evening. The big shock came when I went to someone else's house and the television was on. I found myself sick with scenes that had formerly seemed funny or unimpressive. Now, it was like I no longer had an armor of indifference protecting me. I was horrified by the multitude of opportunities to sin as I simply sat in someone else's living room. Even more alarming was the picture of my small children seeing for the first time scenes definitely not fit for their eyes, with no one else even noticing. We have all been shaken by moments of doubt or thoughts that perhaps the daily fare of television is not healthy for our kids' minds and souls. But how many can do anything about it? There are televisions in the dentists' offices. There are televisions in restaurants. There are televisions in cars and waiting rooms throughout the nation. But are they being controlled by any thinking mind? They are allowed to play on and on with no concern for who is sitting in front of them or what might happen to the soul under its influence.

I can hear the roar of protest, "It is up to parents to watch their kids! The television is not at fault." No, it is not. It is a tool for whoever will use it. The question being asked is: are we using it or are we as a people being used by it? Do we sit like lumps on logs just accepting the fact that a disgusting scene is being offered to us, and we sit by and barely stir?

The palantir has us in its grip. Television can be and is often an assault on the human person as God intends us to be. The very nature of our souls is under constant attack as the virtues are scorned and belittled as little more than a momentary personal choice. When we are faced with violence and danger to our soul we have not only a right to act but a duty to defend ourselves.

Yet, there are examples of great television fare which can highlight the noble struggle of the soul as it strives to become close to the Creator of the Universe. There are programs on television which can and have in fact led many souls back towards God. Television is not the problem. Our weakness in the face of its misuse is the problem. We sit there and accept whatever is on because we can hardly force ourselves to move. We are paralyzed by a strange sort of mental and physical inertia which allows evil to cruise through our living rooms and into the minds of our children. We just figure it isn't that big a deal.

What is true for television is true for computer use. The computer is not an evil box, but it can become the source of great harm to your family if your children obtain access to sites which they should not have. Actually, the sites that are dangerous to our children are usually just as dangerous to us as parents. Nothing that disables the conscience or overrides one's better judgment for the sake of getting some information is good for any of us. Information is not our God.

We remember Adam and Eve and that fruit. There are many times when it seems that we are still chomping away on that fruit from the tree of knowledge of good and evil. We are still in the midst of original sin. We still want to be like God and have all the knowledge and power of God at our finger tips. But we are not God and what we do can either lead us toward Him or away from Him. If we do something to gain power or knowledge that is not for us to have, then we have crossed a line and we are offending Him. It is not good to offend God. We have but one purpose in life and that is to know, love and serve God. No knowledge, no matter how apparently useful to the human race, is worth having if it offends His Almighty Will.

Television and computers are not the problem. Our weakness towards sin is the problem. For some of us that means that we never turn on the tools of temptation, while others can manage to use the tools but avoid the evils. Even under the best of supervision, the devil likes to play games with us. He does not grow weary. He does not get frustrated. He just keeps at us, offering us temptation after temptation. It is up to us to avoid the occasion of sin and to admit when we slip. We are not God. We are human. Poor Pippin had to learn the hard way that simple curiosity can betray us into profound danger. Remember the incident with the palantir when he just wanted to take a little look? He was nearly engulfed by the consuming power of his enemy. We must be self-disciplined. We must fight continuously and when we are weary we must retreat to a safe distance. Television and computers are not a good retreat for the weary. It is always better to keep ourselves in top shape when combating the possible evils which can assault us from the hidden corners of modern society.

It is also a good idea to find something else to do with our time than constantly putting ourselves into the path of battle. It is a very good idea to nourish our souls with the spiritual food of prayer and good counsel and of course the grace of the sacraments. God is with us. He will not abandon us. But we have an obligation not to surround ourselves with things that draw us away and make us ugly in His sight. What do we hold as treasures in our homes? What is the center of our living room and kitchens and bedrooms? Is the Lord welcomed or is rather the television the biggest piece of furniture? Does it dominate the landscape of our lives? Can God's quiet voice be heard over the continuous drone of twenty-four hour news and movie dramas? Is God the center of our lives? If He is, then perhaps it would be good to make Him the center of our living rooms as well.

Medical Technology

"The hands of the king are the hands of a healer. And so the rightful king could ever be known." (The Return of the King)

Aragorn did not need very complicated medical tools and medicines to heal those injured by the grave evil of Sauron's servants. If only King's Foil, the medicinal plant used by Aragorn, could serve us so well. There are many who encourage the use of herbs and natural medicines and though that is quite wonderful, few will argue the fact that modern medical technology has done a great deal to save innumerable lives. It is truly remarkable how serious ailments have now been tamed to the point of being minor inconveniences. What would have been a life-threatening surgery in the past is now little more than an overnight in the hospital. We are amazed. Or at least, we should be.

But there is a reverse side to our success in the medical field. As with other aspects of our lives, so in medicine there must be boundaries to what we do and explore. When we become so consumed with our existence here on this Earth that we forget that this life is not the purpose of our existence then we have skipped over an important line. This takes a tremendous leap of faith for many, but there are times when even medical knowledge should be curtailed for the good of our relationship with God. Let me give a somewhat ridiculous example and it might illustrate the point. What if a man wanted to live forever, and therefore decided that in order to do so he must freeze his body at the first sign of a serious ailment? Then he would have some sort of note attached explaining his condition so that when medical science had developed to the point of curing pretty much everything, including his particular ailment, he could be reawakened and treated successfully. It sounds almost logical doesn't it? Unfortunately that is not in line with the way that God made us. To spend an inordinate amount of time and energy on prolonging bodily life ignores to a sinful degree the very purpose of our existence. We are not here to live forever or to be always happy or to have "the good life." We are here to fulfill the mission that God has entrusted to each of us. This mission necessitates knowing, loving, and serving Him above all things, including our very life as we know it, and facing the fact that our time on Earth is limited.

The truth of the matter is that we will all die. It is part of the natural process of our human experience and one cannot cheat death. God may give us the freedom to fool ourselves, but even that won't last forever. Eventually, we all have to cross the threshold over to the other side. This thought terrifies many people to the point where they will do almost anything to avoid dying. As a matter of fact, any form of physical suffering has come to frighten many a soul, and thus the industry of medical remedies has flourished. I do not condemn the industry itself, for it is responding to a clamoring demand. Pain can and should be relieved when necessary. But we might question the fear which drives this demand. What are we so terribly afraid of? Pain and death are the horrors of this life. Meaningless pain drives people towards a cure at any cost. The black wall of an unknown darkness, which is how many people see death, frightens many out of their wits.

The concept of pain as a form of personal redemption has been lost on many. Gone is the insight that in our suffering we can join Christ on the cross and offer ourselves in complete love to life's hurts and joys. In this we become greater than ourselves, for it takes a supernatural outlook to offer our varied suffering up and to love God deeply in the midst of pain, as we ask for the redemption of ourselves and for the whole world. Only in our sorrow are we stripped of our pretenses and arrogance. Only in suffering do we have nothing to offer except ourselves. Only in our suffering are we free to love without counting the cost. Only when we have said yes to deep loss do we express the kind of love God offered to us when He gave up His only son. When we are hurting beyond bearing and we love God and all His children because He loves them, then and only then are we truly loving as we are asked to love. "Love as I have loved you."

When Frodo was forced to carry the pain of the stab wound from the Nazgul's knife, didn't you ever wonder why Tolkien left him to suffer for the duration of his life? Tolkien could have allowed him to be healed permanently, but he simply let him suffer. Though Frodo knew periods of wellness the wound was always with him. Why? There was a very good reason, I think, and it goes back to the truth of our existence. Suffering is a part of the human experience, and through it we can be drawn closer to God. Nothing teaches us so well our utter dependence on Him and our need to be made whole. We carry within each of us the wounds of sin and brokenness which hurt us even when all seems well. We, like Frodo, are never truly healed until we are united fully with God.

Suffering is such a frightening reality to some that nothing can justify our putting ourselves willingly in its path. Yet every baby born encounters some pain in the process of coming into the world. God does ask a lot of us, yet He gives more than he asks. Suffering is only part of the equation, and it does have a part to play, though we do not always understand it fully. We can refuse to accept life, and we can refuse to accept death; but that won't change reality. We attempt to become our own gods once again. The driving force behind our thought may be that no suffering is worth a risk. It is better to play God than to suffer. This is an interesting process of thought, but entirely wrong. The fact is that Christ commanded us to pick up the cross of our lives and to follow Him. The pains and sorrows of life we have to accept and try to endure. We all need support. The greatest support we can get is from God Himself. He does make His burdens light even while we are calling on His mercy. Suffering and death are quite frightening, especially when they are happening at the same time. But we will be sustained through this, too, and carried into the next world by unseen hands.

Our medical technology has developed to the point where we have to think long and hard when we contribute to experiments that involve questionable ethics. Have we an invitation to do whatever we want? Is it right to expect God to give life in situations where many embryos are conceived so we can use them for experimentation and when those innocent lives are no longer useful to us, we destroy them so as to erase the physical reality of our experimenting with conception? Is God pleased with us when we insist that we have the right to kill a baby in the womb because it will make our life harder or more painful if we carry the baby to full term? Is suffering to be avoided at the peril of our souls? Because we have the power to be a part of creating life, does that mean we have the power to destroy life? God has given humanity freedom to do its worst, and it seems we delight in our power. If we are Christians and profess that God is the author of all life, then we are living a massive cultural contradiction. We cannot say that God is God and then allow our medical procedures to treat life as a commodity which only has value if it is wanted. God takes every soul he creates home to Himself, even though we may never have believed in their supernatural reality.

In *The Lord of the Rings* it is a constant source of wonder that such a little, insignificant people as the Hobbits of the Shire could have been chosen to go on such a perilous mission. And so God has chosen the unwanted "products of conception," the silent, innocent souls of His creation, to bear the cross of our sins as a culture.

But the question is always the same. Who are we? Are we God or are we His? Are we still chomping away on that piece of fruit, insisting that to know more is such a good thing that we need not count the cost? The fruit of knowledge tastes good. It feels good. And sometimes it is good. But there are times in our science when we cross a divide that leads us into the realm of evil. The ring is on our finger, and we are having a terrible time pulling it off. In the process, we are not only hurting the innocent but, worse, we are leading our own souls into the greatest peril possible. We are saying that God does not have to be obeyed, and we can chose evil. Perhaps you deal with such issues with the words, "Well, it's not my business. People can do what they want. I don't want to upset others with my views." God has views. We have to decide every day whose views we support.

The fellowship of the ring was formed because each of those involved knew that the world as they knew it would be a much worse place if the evil which threatened were allowed to conquer. Tolkien personally fought (and supported the allies) in two world wars because he knew that he had a job to do that required his presence and voice. He did not stand on the sidelines wringing his hands because he hated to see good men die for their beliefs. No one wants to suffer, but the saints have been willing to suffer and offer up their lives in witness to the eternal truth of Christ's sovereignty on this Earth. They could see what too many of us have forgotten. We are not called to make peace with evil; we are called to bring the peace of Christ into all lives and that sometimes means speaking about a truth few will accept. It hurts to confront family and friends when they want to live in a way that is contrary to the teachings of God. All Christian churches maintained unity on the value of human life from conception until natural death until very recently. It is not progress which has caused a change in some denominations to accept as a mere "choice" to kill a baby in the womb. The choice is between our will and His.

Frodo suffered, so did Sam, so did Aragorn and so did all the noble characters in *The Lord of the Rings*. Suffering is not a sin. Being physically imperfect makes one no less a soul loved by God. When we face the power of medical science, we are in direct contact with one of the most dangerous forces that the human mind has created. God has let us become "like God" in our own minds, and we act like Sauron when we think that we can justify our actions with our own will. As a nation, we need to think very hard and long about what medical technology is really offering us. To cure an ailment is wonderful, but to corrupt a soul is grave sin. Frodo could not be healed in Middle-earth, but he was to go to a land where he would be perfect once more and know the peace of true joy for ever and ever.

Communication Systems

"It is a lovely language, but it takes a very long time to say anything in it, because we do not say anything in it, unless it is worth taking a long time to say, and to listen to." -Treebeard- (The Two Towers)

When we are confronted with evil, we must assess carefully our ability to defend ourselves and to discern truth from lies. This section will deal with all forms of communication and our ability to speak before we think. It also raises the questions: whom do we listen to most? And who are the authorities in our lives?

Part of the reason that the Shire was such a charming place was because it remained a little off the beaten path. Poor Gandalf was considered a suspicious character simply because he was so different. As Christians, we are called to love everyone and to be willing to hold off judgments while welcoming the stranger into our midst. God was teaching us by example when he told the story of the Good Samaritan.

Yet when the Good Lord sent out His apostles, he warned them to be as innocent as doves and as wise as serpents. In other words, they were to be careful and not swallow the bad with the good. They were to bring the Light of Christ into the larger world and not allow the world to swallow them up. Because we have so many ways of communicating and being brought in contact with others at a moment's notice, then we often do not have a chance to think about what we are saying or what is being said to us. Is it possible that we are becoming the embodiment of the Tower of Babel? Our tongues were created for a very noble reason. Our minds were formed so as to allow us to become great, growing far beyond the beasts of our world. Yet are we even thinking about what we are saying and what we are thinking? Is there any thought to our thought? Are we rushing around telling everyone about our business and taking calls, texting, and hearing so much and talking so much that we are in a constant state of communication overload?

When Frodo needed help, he had to go to a quiet place and think things through. He didn't ask everyone to sort out his problems, and he knew too well that the answer he was searching for was the hard one he had been avoiding. Often, we don't need to talk so much as we need to be quiet. Is it a waste of time to do things more slowly and think our words through first before we make a call?

Do the news commentators, who tell us all sort of things as if they knew the mind of God, know what they are saying? Or are they merely talking so as to keep our attention so we won't change the channel? How many times have we been offered popular lies as truth because a famous person said it? How often have we bought something or done something on no better recommendation than that a pretty or handsome face told us to? Who are these demi-gods who talk to us and try to form our consciences even giving us advice on the most intimate of topics? What training in the teachings of Christ do they have? Are they quoting Scripture? Are they repeating the sermons of the Church Fathers? Are they handing down the deposit of faith? Are they following the lives of the saints? Who are we listening to?

Luckily for Frodo, he was not surrounded with as much confusion as we find ourselves in on an average day. Yet there was a very telling moment when Boromir was trying to convince Frodo to give the ring over to him, and Frodo responded with a significant thought. He said, "Your words would seem like wisdom but for the warning in my heart." We are a people who do not allow ourselves the time and space to listen to the warnings of our heart. We are drowning in opinions and views and arguments of every shade and notion. Evil is frequently presented as good, and good as a foolish and antiquated notion. There is truth and we do carry the power to discern the truth, but it is not something that can be done in a split second every few minutes. We need time to think. We need to nourish our souls on the words of God. We need to be fed by the sacraments of His Church, and we need the help of wise souls to bring light into the darkness. We are not alone, and though the job before us is a hard one, we have been given significant assistance. In the last section of this book I would like to offer the light of Galadriel to each of you. I may not have been created at the time of the Eldar but nevertheless I have access to such as Galadriel offered to Frodo. The fact is that we all do. God is kind and merciful. He is also just. Let us consider listening to those who offer us the light of truth, and retreat for a moment from the din of endless babble.

Chapter Six
Our Heroes and Saints

"The Simarillion is the work of a profoundly religious man. It does not contradict Christianity but complements it. There is in the legends no worship of God, yet God is indeed there, more explicitly in The Simarillion than in the work that grew out of it, The Lord of the Rings. Tolkien's universe is ruled over by God, 'The One'. Beneath who are not gods but angelic powers, themselves holy and subject to God; and at one terrible moment in the story they surrender their power into His hands." (J.R.R. Tolkien: A biography p. 99)

Saints are people who have lived lives of the highest virtue. They may have started out as ordinary sinners, or in some cases as extraordinary sinners; but something happened in their lives when they became completely orientated toward God. Other names for saints are as follows: true Christian, child of God, pure in heart, holy person, martyr, righteous, worthy, pious, full of good deeds, and virtuous. Truly, they are unusual in their extreme devotion and faithfulness to God. No one is born a saint except the Blessed Virgin Mary, Mother of God, and few on Earth rate the title "Saint" before they die. But there are those figures in history and those hidden in our present day who have a holy influence on the world by the way they live their lives. We are all called to be saints; but by its very nature, becoming a saint is a difficult process. In fact it is an impossible one without the assistance of the Holy Spirit. Yet, as Christ tells us in parable after parable, the price is small compared to the reward. We must build up treasure in heaven where no Earthly destruction can bear it away. Many of the characters in Tolkien's books lived lives of high virtue or, as in the case of Faramir; they were of the best quality. They were not looking to be called such; rather, they were responding to a call to fulfill their noblest potential. That is what we are all called to do. In our response, we either ennoble our lives and those around us or we degrade the whole human race. The question for us is: "To be or not to be" ….a saint.

Frodo and Saint Thomas More

" 'I think I know already what counsel you would give, Boromir,' said Frodo. 'And it would seem like wisdom but for the warning of my heart.'

'Warning? Warning against what?' said Boromir sharply.

'Against delay. Against the way that seems easier. Against refusal of the burden that is laid on me. Against – well, if it must be said, against trust in the strength and truth of Men.'" (The Fellowship of the Ring)

Frodo was a character who stood out for his ability to see the truth of a situation and fight to keep that truth in his mind even as he must struggle to destroy the very force of evil which assailed him. In a way, it all seems rather easy. Certainly, he had to leave home and go to strange places and even face terrifying foes; but one never wondered if Frodo knew the truth. We were always assured that Frodo understood the situation clearly, even when others around him were a bit confused. In order to clarify this magnificent struggle, let us look at a real, historical example of a person who fought, much like Frodo, to keep the truth in his heart even as all the world around him was losing its mind.

Saint Thomas More was a man who was well educated, had a very loving family and was doing very well in the eyes of the world. He was the friend of King Henry the Eighth and was considered a valued advisor. Yet when the issue of truth came up Thomas More could not be shaken. The king wanted to divorce his wife so that he could marry another woman. Since it was the Catholic Church which gave Her blessing to the first marriage, and all legal matters concerning the marriage had been addressed, there were simply no grounds for saying that a marriage had not taken place. An annulment could not be granted; thus, a divorce was out of the question. It helps to understand that from the position of the Catholic Church all divorce is condemned by Jesus as not faithful to the covenant bond created between man, woman, and God in the marriage sacrament. An annulment, on the other hand, clarifies that no true marriage took place in the first place. As a solution to his problem, King Henry VIII wanted to place himself at the head of the Church of England and insisted that he would accept no authority greater than his own mind in religious matters. In other words, he was making himself the pope. Now, Christ did give the power and authority of this Earthly kingdom to a man in the role of a servant, and that man was Peter. Following him there has been a continuous line of Popes who have held on to and protected the deposit of faith and furthered the truth of Christ despite personal sin and at times difficult personalities. The question Thomas More was faced with was; who could have the authority of Christ on Earth to protect and explain the teachings of Christ in an ever changing world? Who had the gift of the Holy Spirit and was chosen by God to do His work in this manner?

The king had a very clear reason for wanting to take the authority to himself, but he had no basis for his claim to such authority. The situation was horribly clear in its logical conclusion. The King was committing a grave sin while leading others to stray from the truth of His deposit of faith in the Universal Church. What was Thomas More to do? He could keep his Earthly position and his wealth, and keep his family safe and happy if he but acquiesced to the King's demands. But Thomas knew the truth. He could not blind himself and not see the evil that was being done. He did not want to die and leave his family, but he could not deny the truth of Christ in His Church. So he would not accept the 1535 Acts of Supremacy which gave the title of Supreme Head of the Church of England to the king.

This must have been a terrible time for Thomas More as his own wife and children tried in vain to get him to make peace with the king. They needed their husband and father and yet he not only had to abandon his own life into God's hands, but he had to also resign the care of his beloved family into God's eternal care once he was gone. Saint Thomas More was beheaded on July 6th, 1535. He had written two major works, *Utopia* and *Dialogue of Comfort against Tribulation*. He was not only explaining the truth of faith but he was also lighting up the dark places of the world with his words. His own prayer, which reflected the holiness of his life, says much about what it is that makes a man a living light. "Give me, good Lord, a longing to be with thee: not for the avoiding of the calamities of this wicked world, nor so much for the avoiding of the pains of Purgatory, nor of the pains of Hell neither, nor so much for the attaining of the joys of Heaven... as even for a very love of Thee." His words on the scaffold were poignant as he said, "I am the king's good servant, but God's first."

Saint Thomas More loved God even unto death. Millions of people have read of him and been inspired by his faith. Many people who were confused and lost looked upon the life of this singular man and there found the strength to repent their own weakness in times of trial and tribulation. It takes a saint to make us realize that though God asks a great deal from us; our mission is not an impossible one. He aids us unto the very end and the miraculous can happen. We find that we are not mere individuals but a part of a magnificent whole, a communion of souls who love Him above all and that our communion is not only a gift to ourselves, to the depth of our being, but also a light unto the world.

Sam and Saint Isidore the Farmer

> " 'If you don't come back, sir, then I shan't, that's certain,' said Sam. 'Don't you leave him! They said to me. 'Leave him! I said. I never mean to. I am going with him, if he climbs to the Moon, and if any of those Black Riders try to stop him, they'll have Sam Gamgee to reckon with, I said.' "
> (The Fellowship of the Ring)

Sam was a whole lot more than a sidekick to Frodo. If he had been nothing more, he would hardly have been able to carry out the mission that was entrusted to him. None of us holds a lesser place because we serve others. The ironic thing is that the good Lord seems to choose those He trusts most to carry out the tasks of seeing to the welfare of others. In this world, we seem to think that to be someone's friend means we must align ourselves to the thoughts and feelings of the other rather than to lead them on to the truth which is best for us all.

Saint Isidore lived from 1080 to 1130 AD. You could say he was a man a lot like Sam in that he was a man who knew the Earth well since he was a farmer, and he was from humble origins. He did not go on any great journeys that we know of or help to save the world from the evil of a destructive force. Or did he? Isidore was known as a man of exceptional prayer. He would go to daily Mass and there is a story that when his employer came in anger to denounce him for being late to the field, he was surprised to see a heavenly assistant helping Isidore at a second plow pulled by two white oxen. In another story, Isidore had felt a pang of sympathy for some hungry birds on a winter day, so he poured out half his grain to them, only to be repaid by God when his sack yielded twice its normal amount. These two episodes illustrate more than cute stories about the holiness of an individual. They reflect the awe felt by the people around him who saw miraculous things happen and could only account for them by the intervention of God. What could account for his strange abilities? Why were many more miracles accorded to his intervention even after his death? "In 1211 he is said to have guided King Alphonsus of Castile in a vision to an unknown path, which enabled him to make a successful surprise attack on the Moors." (p. 252 *The Oxford Dictionary of Saints*) One can only wonder if a deep life of prayer can take you even further than modern transportation.

    Sam loved Frodo deeply, but he loved something else besides. He loved the purpose of his mission and the "Hidden King" he was serving. Yes, he had his doubts about Aragorn for a time, but there is the feeling that it was more than the human form of Aragorn that Sam was trying to please. Sam had a notion that he had a mission to accomplish and that it was worth his very life to fulfill that mission. As he said in the movie, "There is good in the world and it is worth fighting for." When one looks at a simple servant such as Isidore, one is struck with the reality that God does choose the humble to confound the wise. Remember how the Orcs were frightened of Sam's shadow and the light that he carried? They could not see his simple peasant body because there was something greater emanating from it, the force of the God who makes us all great enough to die for.

    Sam did amazing things in his desire to simply be faithful. Isidore did amazing things in his love and faithfulness to God and his quiet simple obedience, even to the humblest service of tending to the Earth. Sam and Isidore proclaim a nobility of character in their faithfulness of service. It was Blessed Teresa of Calcutta who said that we are not called to be successful but rather to be faithful. Sam the character knew this and Isidore the saint lived and died this truth. Isidore did the miraculous no less wonderfully than Sam's helping to destroy the ring of power. Who knows how many souls were saved by Isidore's humble prayers and heroic example?

God is not limited to our time on this Earth, and He can choose to work through those He chooses even after they have left the site of their Earthly domain and joined Him in their final reward. We suspect that Sam had work left to do on Earth and that is why he did not sail away with Frodo. Sam had to carry on his role as humble servant even as husband and father and thus he passed on his example into the lives of his children. When Sam dies, we are not there, yet in a way we are. We know that he would be mourned and missed as a man of much love, so he would have been loved by those who knew him. Yet we trust that his spirit would live on, and the adventure of overcoming evil with the witness of his courage in song and story would last for ages to come.

Saint Isidore lived and died over nine centuries ago, yet many who read about the life of this saint are struck by his humble origins and God's choice of him as a hero. We must remember that we have a mission no less great and though the world may not see it and in fact there are those who may scorn our efforts, if we love God and serve Him faithfully, then we are living a life of true holiness.

Pippin and Merry and St. Tarsicius

> " 'It all depends on what you want,' put in Merry. 'You can trust us to stick to you through thick and thin – to the bitter end. And you can trust us to keep any secret of yours – closer than you keep it yourself. But you cannot trust us to let you face trouble alone, and go off without a word. We are your friends Frodo. Anyway: there it is. We know most of what Gandalf has told you. We know a good deal about the Ring. We are horribly afraid – but we are coming with you; or following you like hounds.'"
> (The Fellowship of the Ring)

The portrayal of youth who offer their lives to save a friend is a rather common theme, but in actuality it is a rare event. Both Pippin and Merry care very deeply for Frodo, and in the book this relationship is more drawn out than in the movie, though the movie does a good job of showing their devotion. In the case of these two different Hobbits, they feel a kinship with Frodo that is very much like brotherhood. They know that he needs help but won't ask for it, and they know that they have skills (by their very audacious easy-going-nature) that he lacks. They are willing to follow him through thick and thin even when they haven't a clue what trouble lies before them. It is almost as if they really do not care to know too deeply about the future because nothing could persuade them to leave Frodo's side willingly. At the council at Rivendell, they find a way to plead for a place in the fellowship and, moved by their devotion to their friend, Elrond is persuaded to let them go, even though it is against his better judgment. Only when they are captured by the Orcs and Frodo has run off to complete the mission with Sam do they find the fellowship completely broken. Or at least their physical relationship is broken by distance, but their spiritual ties are as strong as ever in that they are never far from each other's thoughts. In their eventual reunion and throughout the story, Pippin and Merry are seen as two not terribly useful Hobbits who have tagged along to be with their friend. Yet, in the process of each adventure, as they grow, literally and figuratively, they come to find themselves assisting others even if it is in nothing grander than staying by their side. Of course, we know that each has his heroic moment and that they are finally shown to be great Hobbits in their own right but this is hardly necessary, for we have already come to love and accept them as noble souls whose love and devotion make a magnificent difference. At the end they are able to go home, and in their maturity they are able to deal with ruffians and problems which would have daunted them just a year previous. Now, as they carry on their lives, they have won our hearts as well as our confidence that they are good and faithful friends in the Shire who will serve their community well.

Saint Tarsicius was a youth - we are not certain of his age - who lived in the 3-4th century. Though we do not know a great deal about his life, we do know one significant fact: that he died defending the Body of Christ in the Eucharist. He had been carrying the Precious Body when he was waylaid by a pagan mob that killed him with stones and clubs when he would not surrender his charge. Now, here is a heroic example of faith and devotion. First of all, it is a matter of Catholic faith going back to Christ Himself that He gave us His own Body and Blood in the institution of the Holy Eucharist on Holy Thursday. Why else would Christ say that we are to eat of His Body and drink His Blood if he didn't mean what he was saying? Why would he willingly lose so many of his followers if it was a matter of a misunderstanding that He failed to clarify? Christ had a very direct style. He may hint at the future and refuse to tell the end of the world, but he was not shy about explaining who He was and what He had to offer. When He gave His Body and Blood, he did so literally, both on the cross and in the Eucharist. He said so. To argue with this element of Catholic teaching is to argue with Christ Himself. Tarsicius knew exactly who it was he was carrying as he traveled the by-ways of ancient Rome. When a mob tried to get him to give up his Friend he would not. He was carrying the Body of Christ, his deepest love who, though in an apparently helpless state, was none the less the greatest of all in the universe. Was he worried that they could hurt God? Probably not. He knew who God was and is and always will be, but it would be no different if we were carrying the body of a friend. We want to protect that friend no matter what the cost. It would have been a terrible thing for the Eucharist to be desecrated, and Tarsicius was willing to lay down his own life rather than offer up the love of his life. Though we do not know how Tarsicius came to have such a faithful disposition and mature understanding of the life of His Lord, we do know that when it came to the reality of choice, he was willing to make the greatest sacrifice he could.

When we compare these two figures we see two different avenues leading to the same basic conclusion. When we love deeply and sincerely, we are called to go beyond our own selfish desire to protect ourselves, and we reach out with everything we have to save those we love. In our time, the devil has been very successful in combating this commitment of love by whispering lies which assure us, "We must be reasonable and take care of ourselves first. It is never worthwhile to sacrifice for another, because we are then unable to live up to our own potential, and what a sad loss for humanity that would be!" Yet, the ironic fact is that in the very nature of sacrifice, we find our full potential to live as Christ lived.

Every time a pregnant woman is advised that her career, her health, her relationship, her dreams might be jeopardized by the life she carries, she is told the lie that the baby is not worth the sacrifice. She is promised that it is better to be self-centered. But the facts of our faith point to a very different conclusion. We are assured, as faithful followers of Christ that it is in our very ability to sacrifice that we come closest to the perfection which brings us closest to Him who is our greatest good.

If we are living for the world, for this experience of life on Earth, only then the reasoning of the pagans would be true. Be as selfish as possible and preserve your skin at all costs because there is nothing better, and you want to get the most and have the best while you travel around on this Earth. "Eat, drink and be merry..." But if you are a Christian you are struck by a very different motivation, eternal life with God in Heaven. Tarsicius must have believed in Heaven to be willing to leave his Earthly life to protect his Friend. Tarsicius knew for whom he was dying, and he knew that his poor life on Earth was nothing in comparison to the life he would have with his God. Pippin and Merry too seemed to sense that there was more to life than the silly adventures of raiding Farmer Maggot's garden. They were willing to offer up all they had for the better life of being faithful to a friend. What is life worth anyway when we take away self-sacrifice? Then we find ourselves facing a deadly end where nothing could be worth dying for and yet we must die anyway. The very worthiness of our lives is dependent on our willingness to see beyond it to the greatness which lies in the next world, to the Home which beckons us from afar, to the Father who calls to us, who sacrificed His son for us and who waits for us.

Gandalf and Moses

"Before setting off on the return journey to England, Tolkien bought some picture postcards. Among them was reproduction of a painting by a German artist, J. Madlener. It is called Der Berggeist, the mountain spirit, and it shows an old man sitting on a rock under a pine tree. He has a white beard and wears a wide-brimmed round hat and a long cloak. He is talking to a white fawn that is nuzzling his upturned hands, and he has a humorous but compassionate expression……..and long afterwards he wrote on the paper cover in which he kept it: 'Origin of Gandalf'." (J.R.R. Tolkien: A biography p. 59)

Yes, yes, the staff, the long white beard, and the wise look in ancient eyes had a lot to do with this comparison; but there was an element which goes a bit further which is interesting. Moses was a man who had a very unusual childhood and was destined for a holy mission. He was from a poor Israelite family but ended up being adopted and raised by the Pharaoh's own family. He was exiled and went off to a far-away land. Later he returned to lead God's people on a forty-year expedition in which they wandered, being in total dependence on the daily bread that God offers in the form of manna. Moses pulls them along despite their grumbling and leads them to a new homeland. It could not have been an easy task leading these restless people about the desert, and we wonder why the Good Lord had to make them wait so long. But there is a reason and He says so plainly. He is waiting for the old generation of corrupted Israelites to die, and a new, more pure hearted generation to grow up, before He would allow them into the Promised Land. He wanted a purified people who have turned away from their evil ways.

When we look at Gandalf, it is true that we do not know a whole lot about his early life. But we can guess that he has been raised and educated to do great things, even though he might not have realized the extent of it. Gandalf was not top wizard but, as we know, he had the makings of such. He enters the picture in the story of *The Hobbit* to commence a long and dangerous journey so as to help his Dwarf friends regain a lost fortune and an ancient home. He succeeds in that he found someone he could trust to help carry out the mission which would lead the troop through thick and thin and return home again. The second journey in *The Lord of the Rings* demands that Gandalf act as guide and counselor once again. The group is led through much wandering, and time seems to slow down as they experience new worlds and learn new things. None of them are the same when they return to their homes the following year. They are a people transformed in a greatly changed world.

Gandalf, like Moses, is a somewhat reluctant leader who is forced to reach deep inside himself and becomes what he never knew was possible. Gandalf changes from "Gandalf the Grey" to "Gandalf the White". Moses is transformed from an unknown Israelite baby to Egyptian nobility into a Prophet of God. Instead of moving his friends into a new homeland as Moses did, Gandalf helps to change the world so that their homes are safe from the evil which had threatened them. Both leaders find themselves up against rather impossible odds with a somewhat ragtag group who have to become greater than they have ever been in order to safely reach their goal. There are many such stories of groups pulling together to become transformed into a greater whole, but I think that *The Lord of the Rings* does something special that the average story cannot touch. *The Lord of the Rings*, in the figure of Gandalf, seems to tie together the Old and the New Testament.

Gandalf could be looked upon as a prophet of old, offering wisdom and insight, and as a priestly figure, who offers himself in a sacrificial moment, and is thus transformed into one who fulfills the will of God. Gandalf reminds us of the covenant made with Abraham to lead his people to their homeland as well as the sacrifice of Christ on the cross to save his people's souls. God called the Israelites to be His people and then as the Lord revealed Himself through the incarnation of His son so He expanded and fulfilled the covenant relationship with humankind to include all who would follow Him and do His will. Abraham, Isaac, Jacob, Joseph, Moses on down the line to Joseph and Mary are life stories which include the struggle and search to find and do God's will. Jesus' incarnation, growing into manhood, preaching, teaching, healing and leading carries on the process. But Jesus fulfills the old covenant when he sacrifices Himself completely on the cross. God Himself died for us. That is how far He will go to bring us home. That is the greatness of His love. Christ is both Prophet and Priest par excellence.

As a priest dies to self in order to do the will of God and lead his people to Heaven; so Gandalf sacrifices himself in order to lead his people from darkness to light. He offers his life to fulfill his purpose in leading his "people" to the end of their journey. He had to be transformed into a renewed state so as to complete his mission as every priest is transformed through the priesthood. Human beings can only offer back to God what was His anyway. Even when we offer up our lives, we are really offering God's creation back to Him. But God Himself offered what we never could. Only through His saving grace of paying what we could never pay, offering what we never owned, loving as we never loved, could God more fully reveal Himself to us. Moses could offer his life only in a limited sense. Jesus offered himself completely in a mystery which is reflected in the Eucharist and as such we are offered Him in such an intimate manner that we take and consume Him as food for our body and soul. God has revealed Himself to us time and again as both Prophet and Priest who sacrifices Himself to lead us home.

Gandalf served both as prophet, offering wisdom and counsel, and as priest, sacrificing his life and being transformed into a new man to save his people. Our priests experience that dual role as they stand in the person of Christ leading souls into the mystery of the Mass. God is ever with us as he led Moses and the Israelites, and as He came in the person of Jesus Christ, as He comes to us through the Eucharist at the hands of a priest. The healing grace of salvation is ours for the asking.

As Gandalf takes his leave of Sam, Pippin and Merry, he comforts them with the words, "Well, here at last, dear friends, on the shores of the Sea comes the end of our fellowship in Middle-earth. Go in peace! I will not say; do not weep for not all tears are an evil."(*The Return of the King*) And so we take constant leave of our fellow travelers on this Earth but let us live in the peace that this is not the end and there shall come a time when all good men and women will be reunited in Christ. We will journey Home and those prophets and priests who have led us forward, including Moses, will be there waiting for us.

Gimli and Saint Patrick

> " 'Tell me, Legolas, why did I come on this Quest? Little did I know where the chief peril lay! Truly Elrond spoke, saying that we could not foresee what we might meet upon our road. Torment in the dark was the danger that I feared, it did not hold me back. But I would not have come, had I known the danger of light and joy.' " (The Fellowship of the Ring)

Granted, the historical data concerning Saint Patrick are so mixed with legends firmly embedded in the common mind that it may take a moment to give the saint a fair chance to speak for himself. Patrick was born in England and as a child he was kidnapped by Irish raiders. He was forced to live as a slave for many years and tend sheep on the farm of his master. During this time he seemed to have developed an extraordinarily close relationship with God. One day he heard a voice telling him how to escape, and when he followed the advice he was led through an adventure which, though perilous, eventually did lead him back to his home and family. While enjoying the peace and security of his native home, he felt a deep call to become a priest and eventually to return to the land of his enslavement to bring Christ to those who had been his captors. Again he was to overcome many difficulties and he found himself back in Ireland, but this time as a missionary, not as a slave. As we all know, he had great success, though some of the stories about him may encompass the works of several other missionaries who served with and after him. Still, there is little doubt that Patrick had a tremendous long-lasting impact on the people of Ireland. As with many saints, his influence did not die at his death; rather, it increased. God had found a very useful servant in Patrick though he had never been particularly well educated. He was able to make deep inroads into the missionary territory, thus beginning to create one of the greatest Christian strongholds throughout history. It was the endurance and tenacious determination of the Irish monks that virtually saved civilization during the dark ages with their commitment not only to the truth of Christ but to the truth and legitimate power of learning. The monks kept the books and education of mankind in a forward motion when in many other places this was simply not so. St. Patrick was a part of a greater plan that God revealed through time, which we can only see now in part through the layout of history.

Now, Gimli does not strike us as a man of letters and great learning but he too had the power of commitment and endurance which makes many a saint great. Gimli went on a journey to help Middle-earth be saved from a terrible threatening evil. In his simplicity, he thought he could manage the whole affair by simply destroying the ring with a blow of his mighty ax. When he sees the true power of the ring, he is not daunted but challenged to do whatever it takes to destroy the evil thing.

During the course of the journey, he is able to return to a land where his people for generations have been working and had accomplished much. To his horror, he finds not only that the place of their work and home has been laid waste and overridden by evil forces but that even his relatives have been destroyed. He finds that his ancestral home has been invaded and destroyed. In a response similar to that of Patrick, he finds himself drawn towards the commitment to fight the evil which has done this deed. Patrick had to fight the evil in the Celtic religion, which afforded the people of Ireland the desire and fuel to raid and pillage. He found that, in order to be faithful to the God he served, he must face the very evil which had caused him so much suffering, and bring the knowledge and peace of Christ. This is no easy thing to ask a person. It is much easier to go off to some foreign place and fight battles with those whom you do not know and thus try to bring a light into a distant dark place. But it can be far more painful and confusing to try to bring the light of truth and peace to those who have hurt you personally and deeply.

Think what it must have been like for Christ when he tried to return to his native town and no one would accept him. He was God but because of his familiar face and history no one could see beyond the material to the supernatural truth He was bringing. And so it is with us many times. We are called to bring the truth of Christ to those who live with us and to extended family but often they are the last to listen to anything we have to say. The impression we get is that we are too ordinary to be transmitting such extraordinary news or in some cases such demanding challenges. Yet, the truth that we carry is not a personal truth that we have made up, not if we are true and faithful followers of Christ. The minute we decide we can interpret or alter the teachings to fit a situation or make someone feel at ease, so we tend to lose our way as followers, and thus the power of the message is lost. Our family and friends may look at us and say that we are as much liable to sin as they, and that, in fact, we have a known history of sin so we had best not speak about sin and God too loudly. The irony is that few Christians want to do battle with anyone, much less with family and friends, yet because they have learned the truth of Christ's teaching carried down in the deposit of faith and transmitted by the magisterium, so they find themselves in the ticklish position of having to speak about things that can make other people quite uncomfortable. To simply ignore the truth in a world where lies are aggressively encouraged and spread by the population can give a sincere Christian a definite challenge. Whom do we heed? How do we react? To whom are we most responsible? Will the Lord God accept the fact that we simply didn't want to hurt anyone's feelings? But to refuse to say anything when sin is promoted as a social good and a personal freedom while the goodness of God is seen as limiting and somehow altogether too harsh is in itself a grave sin.

Both the figure of Gimli and the person of Patrick had to make a choice. They had to choose between retreating into safe obscurity or going forward on a journey that would lead them into many a painful battle. One would say that Gimli might have had the desire for revenge in his mind, but there was more to his interest than that, for when the fellowship was broken and Pippin and Merry were captured, then the matter of the destruction of the ring fell into the sole hands of Sam and Frodo. Yet Gimli did not flee or abandon his cause. Justice may have been a primary motivation for the character of Gimli and so it can be for us when we fight the evils of our modern age. Often we are not so spurred into action by pure love of God and defense of His truth as we are responding to an immediate hurtful evil, which we wish to put to a stop. When we try to explain our reasoning and argue our case against the thinking of our time, so we find ourselves clinging to the truth of a mighty God who makes truth reasonable and evil a farce of freedom.

God is God and He chooses whom He will to serve Him in the most varied and extraordinary manners. He calls us in the midst of our brokenness and slavery. He calls us when we are devastated by the destruction of all that was dear in our memory, and He calls us when we are weak and sick. Yet, though the challenge He offers us may be great, and we can see no way clear to follow up on His commands, so we must direct our hearts and wills into doing whatever He asks. It is this blind faith and this unreserved acceptance of the fact of our mission that allows the good Lord to use us and do what we could not imagine. We will be called to face hostile enemies and escape the nets of those who wish to ensnare us, but we must run from temptation and revive our spirits in His truth and grace offered in the Church, through His words and sacraments. We are never alone even when our family and friends reject and abandon us, for the spirit of Saint Patrick lives on and the truth of Christ is stronger than all the hellish winds and torrents of the lies and deceptions of the evil one. May we be willing to challenge evil as did the character of Gimli and the man, Saint Patrick, so that we may be strong in Him who is our guide and our light both abroad and in our very homes.

Legolas and Saint John the Apostle

> " 'I do not think the wood feels evil, whatever tales may say,' said Legolas... 'It is old, very old,' said the Elf. 'So old that almost I feel young again, as I have not felt since I journeyed with you children. It is old and full of memory. I could have been happy here, if I had come in days of peace.'" (The Two Towers)

Legolas is a figure who seems to straddle the worlds of Middle-earth and the land beyond the seas. He could well be seen as an angel who does the work of the Lord but for this instance it would be nice to bring him down to Earth a bit and compare him to another remarkable youth who was a bit unusual in his time and vocation. Saint John was the brother of James, and they had been among the first to embrace the fullness of Christ's truth and mission. John, as we all know, was a special friend of our Lord in that he seemed to have the childlike innocence of purity of heart, yet at the same time he had the depth and strength to be present to Jesus as he hung upon the cross in his agony of death. John was a youth, yet more mature than many a soul who lives to ripe old age. John was blessed with a long life and until his dying day he confirmed the truth of Christ's teachings about the truth of the love which burned in his soul throughout his existence.

Legolas is a character who seems to reflect the same childlike innocence of a clean heart and a pure mind; yet he, too, is stronger than we might first imagine. He is gifted with talents to do what no man can do as he is an elf in a world where men are coming into their own. He can see far and can fight bravely. He is not afraid of the spirits of the dead, and he loves his friends with a fierce devotion which is admirable in one who does not need the friendship of men or dwarves. He is even able to transcend the scarred history of dwarves and elves and forge a lasting relationship which would see himself and his friends through many trials and tribulations. Legolas is not one to run from the fight nor is he one to gloat about his prowess. He is capable to the extreme but not boastful.

A saint is a person who works hard to do the will of God and does not take any gifts or grace he receives as a personal possession to be proud of. Humility is a sure sign that a person is on the right path though he may be frightened by the prospects which lay before him. Both the character of Legolas and the real figure of Saint John loom large in our minds as figures that not only accepted the will of God but were at peace with His demands. Each seemed to accept in a certain supernatural manner the truth that God is the Master of all and that in Him one can find the peace and security of a child in his Father's arms. They seemed to be gifted with an exceptionally high level of trust and calm acceptance. This is not something all saints have initially; but as one travels the path of sanctity, it seems that the good Lord in His wisdom likes to bestow this gift on those who follow Him most closely.

For us struggling to find our way towards sanctity, it can seem more than a bit daunting to face such a figure of mature perfection as Legolas or Saint John; but we must remember that in truth there was not perfection of person but rather a perfection of faithfulness which led to a fullness of grace. So, we too are called to unfailing faithfulness; and thus we are transformed almost imperceptibly into the servants of the Most High. Others may look upon us and see what we do not and they may be impressed by a grace we do not fully realize. We may survive the terrors of dark nights and the sorrows of painful battles with our own sin and the brokenness of our sinful world; but we find, as time moves along, that the scourges no longer frighten and intimidate us as they did in the past. We may find that the terrors of the night do not weigh our hearts down with grief; for we see far and are revived by the constant hope of a life yet to come, a world yet to be fully realized and a love to be fulfilled. Our relationship with God grows over time as we mature. We must not look at heroic figures of saints and fear that we are incapable of such great deeds and levels of holiness. We must admit the truth that, of course, we are completely incapable of the transformation that is demanded of us; but that does not make it impossible for God.

The transformation from servant to beloved child is one that takes place slowly in most cases; and we must have the humility to work in secret and even in the dark so as to simply trust that we are growing stronger. God is doing His part in our lives, despite our many insecurities. God is God and nothing is impossible for Him. He seems to like to take the humble and make them the most mature. He enjoys humbling the proud with the modest. He constantly confronts the well-educated and learned with the simplicity of the wise in spirit. God can take the most wretched and sinful among us and transform us into the greatest of saints. We may not start out as a Legolas figure or be known as a Saint John, but we can become the friends of God in His Communion of Saints and enjoy the company of those who will love us for what we are called to be, the embodiment of God's will for us.

Boromir and Saint Augustine

"'Farewell, Aragon! Go to Minas Tirith and save my people! I have failed.'

'No!' said Aragorn, taking his hand and kissing his brow. 'You have conquered. Few have gained such a victory. Be at peace! Minas Tirith shall not fall!'

Boromir smiled." (The Two Towers)

Sinners who turn into saints are something of a hallmark of entertainment, but one must be careful how our modern movie makers twist this concept to fit the agenda of secular thought. Often we will see portrayals of a person who has lived a sinful life suddenly have some startling experience, which awakes the soul to the consciousness of their bad and dangerous ways. They can see the harm they have done and they repent the sorrow they have caused others. This then leads to a conversion which causes a chain of developments in the person's life, and they become good in the eyes of the world. The movie ends with everyone happy and grateful for the return of one who had been lost. This is all well and good. Transformations at this level are worthy to be cheered and encouraged. But there is a deeper reality which is being missed, and it is being missed for a reason. The reason is simply this: that every sin is first and foremost an offense against God. Our secular world will nod its head to the obvious reality of good and bad behavior—though that is getting more and more blurred—but rarely will our Earthbound mentality recognize the fact that every bad act is an offense against God primarily. God is the cause and end of all good, and anything that ignores that reality hurts not only our personal relationship with the Lord of the Universe but also that with all of mankind.

In order for any true and lasting transformation to occur, there must be reconciliation with God. This cannot be emphasized enough. No good works, no matter how zealously achieved, will ever equal the relationship a person has with his God. Sin by its very definition is a breaking of our relationship with our Creator. When we sin, we bring ourselves into the dark places, and we lose the very will to stay close to that which is our greatest good. Brokenness leads to brokenness, and no matter how much we might want to, we cannot fix ourselves. That is the whole truth of Christ dying for our sins on the cross. He knows our broken sinful nature, and he offers himself in perpetual sacrifice so that we may be saved. But we must align our will to His, or we cannot receive His grace and partake of the healing He offers. Sinners, even great sinners, can become saints, even great saints, but it takes more than a change of heart: it takes a sincere act of contrition.

Most people think they know how to be contrite, but the truth is often deeper than we might think. The word contrition in its original form means to be broken upon the rocks, and when we are sincerely contrite we are truly broken upon the rocks. We find that we are shattered. We find that we are broken into pieces, and we cannot put ourselves back together again. Worse yet, no therapist or healer or doctor can fix us up completely. Our salvation from mortal sin comes only through the grace of God and our acceptance of that grace through contrition and repentance. We must make amends through the grace of the Holy Spirit and through the sacrament of Reconciliation. Then and only then can the transformation be made in a lasting form.

Boromir was a figure who, though good in many ways, had a deep and terrible fault. He was willing to grasp what was not his and take to himself a power which was not his to own. He may have justified his sin by saying that he was going to offer it to his father for the good of his people and that they could perhaps save themselves and all of Middle-earth through the use of the ring; but the fact of the matter was that when he should have been offering protection to Frodo, he offered violence and theft. He would take what was not his.

Saint Augustine was not, by today's standards, what would be considered a great sinner. He was a philosopher looking for the truth. He studied and taught and passed from erroneous thinking to erroneous thinking. He was a brilliant man, but he was almost too smart for his own good. His was a case of the intelligent man who could neither see nor hear. His mother, Monica, was a sincere Christian and that meant she was Catholic to the bone. She prayed constantly for her son to be converted to the true faith but he resisted. He was living with a woman and had by her a son. Augustine was not truly satisfied with the situation he was in, but he was not terribly interested in changing his ways. There was no major tragedy to strike the chord of final discontent but rather it was the continual nagging in his mind and heart that he was not on the right track. Saint Monica's prayers undoubtedly helped. Still, even as he grew to know great Christian thinkers and to see the folly of his own life, dedicated as it was to false teachings, he still resisted the final jump from false wisdom to faith. He once acknowledged God enough to tell Him that though he accepted the need to be free from the sin of living with a woman he was not married to, and though he felt the call to celibacy he asked God to, "grant me the grace to live a celibate life, but not yet." Augustine was thoroughly stuck because he saw the truth of Christianity and he could no longer deny God, but he was so used to a life of sin that he could hardly break free.

Boromir was also a man who was so stuck in a sin that he could not easily break free. He wanted to get the ring, and though he fought the temptation for a long time, eventually he was willing to take the matter into his own hands and act violently towards his friend. The problem with sin is that we tend to excuse it with a hundred rationalizations. We insist in our own minds that the sin is not really all that bad or that it is necessary in some way. If you live according to the standards of the world you will often get all the support you need to think this way. "We have to live together because it is more economical. I have to have an abortion because the baby would never have a good life anyway. I have to steal to make ends meet. I have to lie to keep peace. I have to have this affair because I would never be truly happy any other way. I have to divorce my spouse because he is a jerk and deserves to lose me. I have to miss Mass because my kids need to compete in sports, and it wouldn't be fair to expect them to miss games because of my religious beliefs. I can't go to confession because the priest would never understand. God understands me. God will forgive me because he loves me." And so we go on living in sin. The problem is not that God does not understand or that He won't forgive us. The problem is that we do not love God as we should in order to build a deep relationship with Him. We can change, not when we insist that God accept us but when we begin to accept the reality of who God is.

God is the Creator of the universe. He made every star in the sky as well as every leaf on every tree. He knows the lives of all His people all through all the ages and He cares for each soul. He knows when a sparrow falls and He knows when every sin is committed. He sees us as we struggle and He rejoices in our successes. He helps us to get where we are going and He challenges us to remember that He is God and not every other thing that we like to put in His place. God is almighty, all knowing, all powerful. He is handsome beyond words to describe and there is no man or woman born in all the ages who can compare to Him in attractiveness and beauty. He is gentle, yet stronger than the gravity which holds our Earth in place. He is kind, yet justice is always at hand. He loves us unto death and beyond. He is the greatest person in our lives and yet we ignore Him and place so many trite and meaningless baubles between Himself and our hearts. Truly we must cause Him to suffer deep pain.

Beginning to see God for who God really is transforms us, and we find ourselves falling in love in a way that has never happened before. No human being could call forth and encompass the love that God draws from our souls. To love God is to meet an eternity of joy. This is what happened when Saint Augustine gave up the fight and began to accept God for who He is. He found himself contrite, broken to pieces, and the good Lord picked him up and put him back together again even better than before. He was a new man. Hence the term "Born Again." From that time on, Saint Augustine rose to an understanding of faith which was so outstanding that he is still a model today. He became recognized as a saint by the Catholic Church, and miracles have been attributed to his intervention. His was a life that went from sinner to saint in a remarkable manner, but it is not terribly unusual for the good Lord to show such mercy to great sinners. The Lord has a soft spot, it seems, for those of us who have sinned terribly, and he likes to show the world what He can do with a tattered rag of a soul. Only God can work such transformations.

Boromir was a man who refused to see his sin until he had hurt someone that he had promised to protect. The price he had to pay was to suffer the arrows of evil orcs in an attempt to make up for his wrongdoing. He offered himself in a poignant manner by trying to save the Hobbits, Pippin and Merry, though he could no longer do anything to help Frodo bear the weight of the ring. He had to accept the finality of death and failure as he watched those he was trying to save being borne away by his enemy. Yet, when Aragorn came to comfort him in his last moments, it was then that Boromir showed the completeness of his transformation when he acknowledged the rightful kingship of Aragorn and not his father or himself. He said he would have been proud to serve such a king and in that offering he made the greater sacrifice. He was admitting not only his mortality, which is rather obvious when one is full of arrows, but he was admitting his true place on the Earth and in his whole life. He was never meant to be a ring bearer or to wield great power. He was the son of the steward and that was his place, to serve and to serve faithfully. In his last sacrifice, he demonstrates his willingness not only to acknowledge but also to fulfill that role. He is broken to pieces and in that short time of dying he is put back together, despite all the wounds, into a new man. He becomes whole as he had never been whole. He becomes what he was sent to be.

Whenever we acknowledge the role that God has given us to play, even if that is a role we would like to refuse, we are in the process of accepting the transformation that God offers us from mortal to immortal. Only God can offer us the immortal destiny that He has planned for us. In sin, we break away from that plan by deciding that we know better than God. In reconciliation, we are broken into pieces, and we allow God to put us back together as we were meant to be.

Faramir and Saint Thomas Aquinas

" 'We are truth-seekers, we men of Gondor. We boast seldom, and then perform, or die in the attempt. Not if I found it on the highway would I take it I said. Even if I were such a man as to desire this thing, and even though I knew not clearly what this thing was when I spoke, still I should take those words as a vow, and be held by them.'" (The Two Towers)

Faramir was a very noble character in the book. He was actually far more interesting from the standpoint of a character that did not even have to struggle for wanting the ring as did the movie figure with the same name. There was so much more development of this character in the book that for him alone the book would be worth the reading. Faramir was a man who saw worth in the higher thoughts of men. He was someone who could see his position more accurately than most. He knew that the mystery of the ring was not his domain, and when he learned the secret of who Frodo was, he saw only the greater purpose which led Frodo on such a perilous journey. He had no thought of trying to attack and steal what was not his to have. As he said, even if the ring had been offered freely, he would not have wanted it for it was a destructive thing which would ruin the lives of all who touched it.

Now, there have been many men who have been held up as heroes in our day and for the most part they are fallen mortals who have realized their mistakes. Through the experience of hard knocks, they have come to realize that the false treasures they sought after were indeed leading them astray from what was good and noble in their own lives. These recovered folk have the courage to try to make reparation by speaking honestly about their experiences so that others are not so tempted to be led astray in the same way. They often offer hope to those who have gone off the path and highlight the road to recovery. There are great reasons to support the testimony of such individuals, but there is a loss in our society when we refuse to listen to those who have not fallen so far as if they have nothing to say or offer. The thinking seems to be that unless you have fallen into grave sin you do not really understand it or have much to say on the topic. But that would be a direct contradiction of the teaching of our Lord, who Himself was the greatest teacher and was without sin. He pointed to the faithful son who did not leave his father's side while the prodigal son had gone away and returned repentant. He was not the lesser son for not having squandered his father's money and repented. He was the leader son doing what all good sons should do. He was busy being faithful and hardworking, and his father never lost sight of that in his eagerness to reclaim the lost son. There tends to be a dismissal of those who are not experienced in the ways of sin, as if they have refused to sin out of some weakness rather than thanks to the strength and grace which kept them pure.

Saint Thomas Aquinas was a very unusual fellow in that though he was very smart, he tended to be rather quiet and shy, thus was considered somewhat stupid. He was also very holy and wanted to keep himself pure from sin as much as possible. Because of his unusual capacity to know and love God, the Lord granted him not only an exceptional education but also a high measure of sanctity. His own mother opposed his attempt to join the mendicant order of the Dominicans but as he discerned this to be God's will for him, he would not be dissuaded even after being beaten by his brothers and locked in a room for two years. Eventually his family became reconciled to his vocation, after he stole away, and they came to see him in later years as a holy man who was called by God.

When he went to school, several of the students watched his heavy frame as he lumbered about the university and they considered him so slow and stupid that they named him the "Dumb Ox." He did not seem to take offense but continued on in his usual manner. There is a story which illustrates his great level of sanctity when he was a student. It turned out that some students wished to make fun of him by proving what a simple mind he had, so they called to him in his room and yelled out that there was a pig flying in the air outside his window. Thomas came to the window and to the delight of his fellow students he looked around in the air as if searching for the flying pig. They laughed and scorned him until he said in his quiet and mild manner, "I would rather believe there was a flying pig than to believe that a Dominican could lie." You can imagine the rest. Of course, we know that Thomas went on to write some of the most famous and deep theological works ever presented by man to God. For Thomas always presented his work to God in the Blessed Sacrament, and near the end of his life he was given a vision in which he saw many great things of God, and he came to the conclusion that his works, though great by the standards of men, were only as straw compared to the things of God. He never finished his last great work, though what he left us has been the textbook par excellence for centuries.

Both the character of Faramir and the reality of Thomas show us different versions of a pure mind and heart that does not desire the things of this world. They are the examples we should look to first for they show us an uncorrupted path, and they are the ones we should offer to the pure innocence of our children. When we tell our children that they should respect this or that movie star because they have recovered from a long list of sinful situations or we offer a sports star who is trying to put his life back together after having nearly destroyed himself with drugs and alcohol, should we not consider the fact that we are missing the greater examples which exist all around us in their quiet holiness? There are those persons who have been perfecting their habits and dispositions toward the goal of Heaven since they were children, and they do not search after the baubles of this world's glory or money. These people we might tend to think are less refined and less exciting, and they might talk too softly or chat too simply for our taste. They might repeat themselves and they might not look so beautiful or handsome. They might be very old or they might have the worn look of those who have spent themselves in toil. Often we tend to overlook the characters that we should pay the most attention to. Often we tend to overlook the people who have the most to offer us in terms of examples of holy lives.

We need to consider to whom we listen. Faramir was a good character worthy of more notice than is generally given to him. Yet that is often the way. There is a false estimation that good people tend to be a bit less interesting than those who have lived with more brokenness; yet, as the character of Faramir and the person of Saint Thomas show us, their lives were hardly simple and without excitement. They led incredible lives of varied action and personal adventure, though the adventure may have been more in the spiritual realm at times. Still, the battles a man or woman endures to keep his or her soul pure in the eyes of God can never be really boring if one only considers all that is at stake. The more interesting life would be he or she who has fought on bravely day after day while no one else noticed. Would that we fully understood the spiritual battles we fight each day and presented to our children the noble lives of holy souls.

Eowyn and Saint Clare

"Then the heart of Eowyn changed, or else at last she understood it. And suddenly her winter passed, and the sun shone on her.

'I stand in Minas Anor, the Tower of the Sun,' she said; 'and behold! the shadow has departed! I will be a shield-maiden no longer, nor vie with the great Riders, nor take joy only in the songs of slaying. I will be a healer, and love all things that grow and are not barren.' And again she looked at Faramir. 'No longer do I desire to be a queen,' she said." (The Return of the King)

Eowyn was a woman who was not content with her role as niece of the king. It wasn't that she was looking for glory as much as she was searching for purpose. She saw herself as more than simply a woman who filled a position in society. She was a soul trying to account for herself in a world where it seemed only men did the noble deeds and fought the great fights of life. She was lonely and struggling to find her value as both a woman and as a human occupant of the world. Her decision to disobey her uncle, the King, was tantamount to refusing to live in her natural station in life. She felt she had a different calling and that she must do more than wait at home for the doom of evil to befall her people. Of course, there is much to be said for those who stay at home and keep the fires burning for returning warriors, but she felt a definite call to something different.

In our modern world, it seems that pretty much every woman is called to live the life of a super being. As mothers, we are to be both nurturers and good disciplinarians. As homemakers, we are to provide nutritious meals while keeping our homes in condition to be portrayed by any number of women's magazines. As wives, we are to be both intimate lovers and also the best of friends to our spouses. And then there are those who work outside the home and have careers which pull in a myriad of directions, all claiming that the need to be excellent in our chosen field is the measure of our worth. The case is nonetheless distressing for men who must be all things to all people: wise, sensitive, strong, handsome (or at least mighty attractive), productive and hardworking. The list could go on depending on your personal tastes. We all feel a need to be something more than simple, normal people living ordinary lives. We know that for the most part we can't do much more than be ordinary people striving to do our best, but that does not always satisfy our appetites.

There is a difference between a calling and discontent. A calling by God leads us on to do His will even in the simplest and most ordinary of daily events. Discontent is a continual search for something to fill an aching emptiness which we cannot define. Discontent is often associated with the need to fulfill His will but through a desire to follow our own whims. As we strive to answer the voice of our Lord, we have to contend with many issues. The first is to ascertain whether we are truly called to make a change or deepen our commitment with a specific action, or whether we are simply bored with life and looking for a little excitement. Our unhappy feelings may not stem from being on the wrong path as much as not having the right will. We may be doing what we are supposed to be doing in all its perfect regularity and unexciting nature, but we have lost - or actually never had - the will to do it. For example, if the good Lord has given us a family to look after, and now it seems that the chores of family life are unfulfilling, it might not so much mean a calling to another way of life as to a deeper look into who we are as children of God and the value of how we are called to become citizens of Heaven. Perhaps we are doing great things and we do not realize it. Or perhaps we are doing only what satisfies our emotional comfort zone while we should be considering the destiny God has planned for us.

The issue may not be as much what we are doing as with what intention we are living our lives. We were created to be more than emotional containers forever needing to be filled by satisfying experiences.

When we get to a point where we can say our lives must be centered on God and He must be our greatest love, then a change inward as well as outward is sure to occur. We may or may not be recognized as great by the world but that is of little consequence in the larger scheme of supernatural reality. What the world considers great one day may be old news by the next day. The calling to do God's will is of far greater interest to our souls. And in fact, the response to a call might actually put us into conflict with the people of this world, for the fact is that following the Lord God closely often leads to questions and concerns by others who either do not understand the sincerity of our motives or are threatened by the consequence of our actions. There are those who find God's call restrictive and oppressive. They would rather be free to make their own mistakes and follow their own paths rather than listen to the word of God in revelation of Word, Tradition, or Sacrament. Theirs is a world where the highest good is personal choice and the sight of someone doing the will of the Holy Spirit who leads through law and word is not acceptable.

Eowyn was a woman who did not want to follow the role that had been laid out for her; but there was an understanding that she was not listening to the voice of unrestrained freedom, but rather to the inner call to do a task which was laid out for her. She had to risk the displeasure of those she loved in her uncle and brother to do the will of the secret voice which was calling her. As we know there was a job that needed to be done and only she could do it. No other woman of that place and time would have had the skill, bravery, opportunity and materials at hand to do what she did. She had been trained from youth to become the instrument of the One who directed her to such a terrifying and great deed.

Clare was a young woman who lived in a time not unlike that of the Hobbits. The people did not have the sophistication and advanced technology we know today. They lived without the wonders we consider necessities. She was a woman who was expected to obey her father and then her husband as lord and master. She would not have had the opportunities for education that men would have had. In fact, her whole world would be her family and home.

Clare, at the age of eighteen, was strongly influenced by the preaching of Saint Francis of Assisi. She soon declared her wish to live a life similar to that of the men in the Franciscan order. It took some time and arrangement but she was, within a relatively short period of time, allowed to take the habit of a nun and renounce all her worldly possessions. She was in formation at a Benedictine convent until Francis was later able to offer her and her companions a house. She later became abbess of a community of women who wanted to live as Francis and his companions did in both rule and spirit of sincere, Earthly poverty. Clare lived in her convent for the rest of her life and was a remarkable example of holiness to all those who knew and followed her example including several members of her own family.

Here was a woman who felt a call from God, and despite initial opposition of her family, she was able to fulfill the mission the Lord had set out for her. She was truly a hero in the first degree. She lived a hard life of virtue which demanded more from her personally, physically and spiritually than any mortal will ever be able to accurately account. She, like the character of Eowyn, had to be submissive to the wishes of the Lord God Almighty and put her entire life, reputation and happiness into His hands while stepping carefully outside the expected bounds of her social place. To obey a higher call is often to risk ridicule and misunderstanding because God never calls a person to a life of ease and luxury. He has a long-standing habit of calling people to the very highest levels of human perfection in living out the virtues and avoiding the sins of this Earthly life. Eowyn was lucky in a way, for she was able to recover the loss of her composure and the temptation towards the sin of covetousness, through the realization that she was not meant to marry Aragorn. She was lead to a life more fulfilling than any she could have tried to contrive herself, in her acceptance of the deep and virtuous love of Faramir.

Saint Clare was lucky also, but we would need to use the word blessed here, for the hand of God was definitely upon her. She was able to accomplish greater works in her life of renunciation and gained a reputation for such holiness that she was declared a saint only two years after her death by the Catholic Church. There was no way her life, apart from complete acceptance and absolute love of the Lord's will, could have led her to such heights. Of course, as anyone in religious life knows, she was both a wife and a mother in that she was the mother of her spiritual children who were as Jesus Himself taught, "Who is my mother, my sister, my brother, but he that does the will of my Father." She was also the devoted and most intimate spouse of the Lord God Himself. One does not reach to the stars and truly grasp them as she had done without the will of God. No one does the impossible without a bit of help.

For most of us, our vocation to the will of God will not take us face to face with the king of the Ring Wraiths, nor will we be able to found an order of such great holiness. But that in itself does not much matter. The greatness of our mission is not measured by the results of our actions in Earthly numbers or by the weights of popular opinion but rather by the adherence to the will of the God who created us and directs us. By our fruit we shall be known, and the garden we are sent to tend may be a small plot of humanity in the form of our own family and friends. It may not sound impressive, but if we can witness faithfully our abiding love of God to those He has sent to us, then we will have achieved much though the world measure it as little. I am sure that as Clare sewed in her humble room and performed her simple duties, she saw not the world's esteem or the glory which would be hers in the name of sainthood, but she saw one thing only, her love for her Master, and it ruled her heart and served her mind as well.

We read about Eowyn and we see her struggle with the many oppressive forces which assail her spirit, and only by the gift of having read the book or seeing the ending of the movie do we know the final result of all her pain and endurance. But we do know she will come out of the whole scene of madness in war as someone who has conquered not only the evil passions of the terrible ring wraith, but also her own disordered passions. She submits her will, and she is released into a joy she had never previously imagined. So it is with us. Though we do not get to see the end of the movie right now, so to speak, we live by the faith and hope that we shall be satisfied one day, not on this Earth perhaps but in Heaven, forever with our Beloved in the greatest joy.

GALADRIEL AND THE COMMUNION OF SAINTS

> " 'I it was who first summoned the White Council. And if my designs had not gone amiss, it would have been governed by Gandalf the Grey, and then mayhap things would have gone otherwise. But even now there is hope left. I will not give you counsel, saying do this, or do that. For not in doing or contriving, nor in choosing between this course and another, can I avail; but only in knowing what was and is, and in part also what shall be. But this I will say to you: your Quest stands upon the edge of a knife. Stray but a little and it will fail, to the ruin of all. Yet hope remains while all the Company is true.'"
> (The Fellowship of the Ring)

Galadriel is so strange a figure that it helps to know that she has a long history of doing good and that she is older and wiser than most other characters. She is something of a shadowy figure for all the brilliant white dress and lights of insight and all. The mystery which envelops her is not unlike that of the mystery which surrounds those who live on in Heaven still helping us through the grace of God. We do not know a whole lot about what goes on after our time here on Earth is completed, but we have a sure knowledge that we are at this moment either striving toward joining the saints or breaking away from them. The whole subject of judgment and God's mercy and justice could take another book and is beyond the scope of this little meditation. But what happens to those who have gained entry into the Beatific Vision is something we can tackle, though, obviously, in a limited fashion.

Galadriel was a princess who helped to battle the terrible evil of Morgoth. She lived from the first age into the second where she became queen and founded Lorien. She was able to protect Lorien for, in her power, she knew the mind of Sauron, but her mind was closed to him. She found the opportunity to grasp the ring of power as simply another test of her will against that of the evil which was trying to enslave Middle-earth. Her will was not to become evil but to accept her fate as a part of a disappearing age. She would have to say goodbye to one world in order to embrace a greater life which was her final destiny from the beginning of time.

The souls which inhabit our bodies are so close to us that we often forget that we have them. We forget that we are immortal beings who will have to leave this Middle-earth to accept an everlasting life somewhere else. The Communion of Saints are those who took the reality of their souls very seriously. In fact, they renounced everything that would distract and distance them from that which would harm the life of their souls. We cannot really understand what the world beyond this one is like but we can speculate a bit.

The saints live in a world where there is no longer any pain and they can never sin again. They don't offend God or each other. They don't get sick or get hurt. They don't suffer from any evil or have to fear anything. But better than not having to deal with loss or pain, they experience a host of goodness that is beyond our comprehension. The saints know a great deal more than we do, and they have the freedom to experience knowledge without corruption. They live in a state where everyone gets along, and one can go up and meet any other saint as they wish. A conversation with Moses or Abraham would not be impossible. There is no time limitation, so one could relax without the relentless pressure of the passing moment. Food is no longer a necessity but it could be a source of satisfaction to eat what one liked. Sleep is not necessary, but rest would be constant. They can understand all the mysteries of life, such as why did my brother have to die so young. The lion can rest alongside the lamb. In Heaven, one can walk through a zoo and enjoy the wonderful gifts of the Creator's vivid imagination and boundless exquisite skill. Fences are not needed.

Space is no longer a limitation. Want to travel to India? No problem. An Alaskan journey? Not impossible for the Earth is recreated in all its original perfection. But all these musings are nothing in comparison to the reason that Heaven is Heaven. A saint is in the actual, physical presence of God in such a manner that God's face can be seen and adored. The saint need not sit on a stool and simply stare as if at a picture for the reality of God invites conversation, interaction and experience. The saint lives with GOD. The God who has existed for all of time. The God who created everything from nothing. The God who knows and loves every person who has ever lived and knows all who will yet be born. The God who cares for each sparrow and gives life to each blade of grass. The God who keeps our hearts beating and knows our every thought. The God who has not destroyed this sinful world with its wars and corruption because He can make good come from evil. The God who made a covenant with Abraham and who led Moses and directed, protected, and served His people throughout all of history. The God who sent His only son as a baby to the maid He had fashioned as a second Eve, the Ark of the New Covenant. The God who grew to a man among us and died a tortured death to demonstrate just how far He would go to love us. The God who promised to return and who will bring perfect justice with Him. The God who will live forever. The God who wants us with Him in the Heaven He has created for us.

There is no one that compares to the beauty, ingenuity, nobility, glory and wonder that is Our Lord. We may be free to do a whole lot of wonderful things in Heaven, but nothing will ever compare to being with HIM. The companionship of God is the single greatest thing that can happen to a human soul. Realizing that is the second best.

If we live on this Earth as if we are our own masters, and our needs, desires and whims are of utmost importance, then we will not be able to stand the company of the saints who have put God first. We will not be able to look God in the face. We will not want to take anything more from Him. Our end will be simply a culmination of our lives.

Many saints have rejected the power and glory of being great on this Earth and simply lived quiet lives of seclusion. They helped others despite risk and suffering, and they fought the noble fight when it was their place to do so. They offered their lives and their deaths for something that was greater than themselves.

Those who live in Heaven and form the Communion of Saints are some incredible people like the saints I have mentioned before and other noble souls who have had the grace to be recognized by the Universal Church as saints. There will also be among them those souls who were completely unknown by the larger world but could gaze with love into the eyes of the One True God. To meet His gaze will be the richest reward a human soul can know.

Aragorn and the Hidden King

*"All that is gold does not glitter,
Not all those who wander are lost;
The old that is strong does not wither,
Deep roots are not reached by the frost.*

*From the ashes a fire shall be woken,
A light from the shadows shall spring;
Renewed shall be blade that was broken:
The crownless again shall be king."*
(The Fellowship of the Ring)

Aragorn was a man who was born with a great mission on his shoulders. He did not strut around like some fellow fully aware of his own importance. Rather he acted like someone who felt the burden of tremendous responsibility. He had a lot of humble work to do before he could ever feel the crown of kingship upon his head. In fact, he was extremely reluctant to assume any position of honor, as he was so fully aware of his own humanity and the weakness toward sin which led his ancestor to commit the crime which followed mankind throughout Middle-earth history. Aragorn was given a chance to try to right a wrong by being faithful and humble as his predecessor had been vain and proud.

He had been raised in a relatively safe environment under the care of the elves in Rivendell. When he came of age, his true identity as heir of Isildur was revealed to him. Since he was of the Numenor line, he lived an unusually long life. For some seventy years he served in the wild, fighting the servants of Sauron. He became a very strong and wise man and gained the friendship of Gandalf. It was in the service of Gandalf that he came in contact with the Hobbits and learned the secret of the lost ring of power. He became Frodo's friend and advisor throughout their journey until the break-up of the fellowship.

There are many facets of Aragorn's life which make him an interesting character to study, but the greatest is the fact that he symbolizes the role of the "Hidden King." Obviously, he is not supposed to be the figure of Jesus Christ as both God and man but he is a figure of great nobility and holiness who must remain hidden until the time of fulfillment comes.

Often there is a sense in our society today that Jesus is nothing more than a historical figure. Granted, many will admit that Jesus lived and walked upon the Earth and that he was great and truly the Son of God. But it seems as if, for many, their relationship with Jesus dies at that point. It is as if the figure of Jesus cannot span the great time of waiting, and the hidden form of God is almost too well hidden for many to see. That is why Aragorn becomes a fascinating figure. In him we find the worth, nobility, and reality of someone who must be hidden in order to accomplish a great good.

Jesus lived upon the Earth for thirty-three years. Before he was born, the Israelites had been waiting for approximately three thousand years for their savior to appear. They had known of the existence of God through their fathers Abraham and Moses and through kings like David and Solomon and prophets like Elijah and Elisha. They had many wondrous examples of the Lord's power throughout the lives of Patriarchs and the freeing of the slaves from Egypt. The Almighty made His all-knowing, all-powerful presence known throughout early salvation history. But yet when Jesus finally arrived on the scene, many of the Jewish authorities did not recognize Him because they did not expect Him to humble Himself in the form of a man, much less a baby born of a woman.

For thirty years, Jesus lived alongside mankind and shared the life of a humble servant. Then as he began His ministry and began to teach and perform great miracles, still many of those who had been waiting for Him were blinded to the truth of His message and the reality of His presence. His very closeness was the cause of His not being recognized. Because God is so great, many could not believe that He could be so close to us. Then, as Christ offered Himself on the cross, He demonstrated for one and all how much He loved all of mankind and to what lengths He would go to forgive our transgressions against Him if we are but reconciled to Him. He would die a terrible death to save us from eternal death. The Apostles who knew Him intimately and those who loved Him from a slightly greater distance were all confounded by His death, even though he had foretold it and warned them of His eventual sacrifice. He was the Lamb that would take upon Himself the sins of the world. In the very awesomeness of this message, He was hidden again in a manner of speaking. This incredible news was enough to confound the human mind and overwhelm the human heart. When He appeared again, after the resurrection, He came to those who knew Him, and he revealed Himself as if by continually taking off a shroud of mystery, a disguise of sorts. Always the minds even of those who knew Him well and loved Him profoundly were thrown into confusion at His appearance. He is a God who seems to like to reveal Himself in stages and after periods of being hidden.

We know that He left for all of mankind the Holy Spirit in the Universal Church. Her imperfect human servants try to fulfill the tasks of protecting and explaining the faith which Jesus left to us. Yet, as Jesus is still alive and the Church is the living embodiment of the Holy Spirit, then He has not left us at all but carries on His mission to draw us to the Father through a new but hidden form. The greatest gift He left was His very presence in the sacrament of the Holy Eucharist and in this He is again present but hidden.

God is alive and lives among us, yet, because He is hidden, we tend to almost ignore His reality on Earth. The very scandal of hiding Himself in the Eucharist causes many to discount the truth of His words, but it is well within God's prerogative to do thus. There seems to be a perfection of faith that takes place when we as humans are forced to accept God in a hidden and humble form. In some ironic way it seems to humble our own selves to realize that we must accept God as food and drink, as a man dying on a cross, as a baby, as a promise and as a covenant handed down for thousands of years.

In the Great Almighty's wisdom, we are perfected in our faith when we discern the love of our lives through many veils. We too have a job to do and that is to search for our God, and that means from within as well as from without. We are not born to sit and wait for the Lord to save us, but we are to align our wills and our lives to His perfection. We are asked to live lives of humility and in a way to hide ourselves as he did by loving Him yet not grasping at the greatness of such a union. Our love must ever be that of the child for a beloved parent, as the love of a spouse for her soul mate, of the human being for his Creator. We are blessed because God exists and He saw fit to bring us into being. We are blessed because He loves us and even though we are weak and sin over and over again, He loves us always till the end of time and He will never reject us. Rejection is all on our side when we choose another in His place. We will never know happiness or completion without Him, yet we must practice the virtues which lead us to Him.

Bilbo had no idea what was going to happen to him when he stepped outside his door. He only knew that he was leaving safety and security behind. He knew he was saying goodbye for a time to pleasant breakfasts, leisurely lunches, and hearty dinners. In his journey he discovered much about the world and about himself. He faced evil on a level he had never known. He was forced to overcome his attachment to evil and, in letting go of the ring, he took on the years of natural aging which the force of the ring had dismissed. Frodo carried with him the wound of evil which he had carried for so long, and only in leaving Middle-earth would that wound be healed. All the characters were affected one way or another by the evil of the ring, and only those who had refused its power were able to live on in relative peace after its destruction.

Evil blinds us to God's presence in our lives. We are a wounded people who have been terribly afflicted by the evils which surround us. Only those who have rejected the various evils on Earth are able to claim peace, for it is only in a close union with God that we can ever know His peace. Those who have suffered the effects of personal evil done to them or evil they themselves have committed have but one choice and that is to go to the Great Physician.

It is interesting to notice that Tolkien made Aragon a healer who could undo much evil with his touch and medicine. So it is with God in the person of Jesus Christ. Yet we have to recognize our illness and be willing to bring our wounds into His presence. He can do little for us if we insist on staying in the midst of the very forces which cause us so much harm.

The tragedy of our society is that when a priest or a clergyman from any denomination tries to bring the teaching of Christ out into the open, he is often accused of being judgmental. When a sin is called a sin in our society, there is a loud gasp of horror that a person has committed an incredible act of indiscretion. Yet the opposite is true. To ignore sin and to appear to accept sin is to do the worst thing imaginable. It is like knowing that a person is fatally ill and if they would only go to the doctor they could be healed, but the sick one does not want to face the pain of true healing, so they pull away in anger, and thus the attempt to heal is given up. It is natural to be afraid, but it is wrong to be angry at the one who loves and esteems our worth so much to risk our anger so as to pull us towards that which is our best good. It is wrong to stop trying to encourage others towards God because they will be upset for a time. Trust in the Hidden King to help us all to find Him and be healed once and for all time.

Chapter Seven
Summary

"At last the three companions turned away, and never again looking back they rode slowly homewards; and they spoke no word to one another until they came back to the Shire, but each had great comfort in his friends on the long grey road.

"At last they rode over the downs and took the East Road, and then Merry and Pippin rode on to Buckland; and already they were singing again as they went. But Sam turned to Bywater, and so came back up the Hill, as day was ending once more. And he went on, and there was yellow light, and fire within; and the evening meal was ready, and he was expected. And Rose drew him in, and set him in his chair, and put little Elanor upon his lap.

"He drew a deep breath. 'Well, I'm back,' he said." (The Return of the King)

Tolkien knew this world well and that may be why he chose to write in the fantasy form as he did. He knew that to preach would be to set himself up as a target for anger. Perhaps he felt that the wisdom built into each heart would be great enough to see the message of faith and truth which he so poignantly demonstrated. Tolkien also simply liked to tell a good tale, and it is in the nature of a good story to reflect the truth of our existence on this Earth. It is God's magnificence which enables fiction to reveal the truth in such a fascinating way. Sometimes we can see the mystery of our hidden God better through a good story or an apt poem than through the discourse of theologians.

Our God is a Hidden King, and we are blessed that there are many who love Him so deeply that they reveal His truth in a myriad of ways. Saints practiced the virtues we discussed earlier. They were called to manifest the glory of God on Earth in some fashion, and they all fulfilled their quest. The key was not their strength nor their attractiveness nor their innate intelligence. The key for all of them was the depth of their love. To know God is to want to love and serve Him with all your heart and all your mind and all your soul and to want to draw others to Him.

The Lord of the Rings was a profound book on many levels and I have touched but some of the spiritual aspects. There are those much better qualified to amplify or deepen the threads which I have touched upon. Yet the grace I have received while considering just the points I have mentioned have been tremendous. Our lives are enriched by such musings, and it is good to take the time to consider what we watch, read, and with whom we speak, in terms of how much they draw us towards the greatest good of our lives.

We must take time out during our busy lives and consider the place that God has in our lives. Tolkien's gift was that he never had to even mention God's name yet we are drawn with his charming writing skills towards thoughts of God and His creation. Tolkien ended his great work with Sam returning to his home and family. It was a beautiful ending. It is what we all want in our deepest longing. We want to be home with our family. It will be the best home in the universe and our family will be far more wonderful than any we have ever experienced here on this Earth. It is worth practicing the virtues until we are exhausted. It is worth turning away from the temptations of every sin. It is worth living for. It is worth dying for.

May God grant every reader the strength to face the evils of the Mordor in our midst, to throw the rings of power far from ourselves and our families, and climb upwards despite our fears, enduring every challenge He sees fit to set before us. May He offer us the wisdom of guides who serve Him well and gain the refreshment of resting in the peace of prayer. May we one day sail to the Home He has promised us if we but follow Him.

"We have come from God..."
—*J.R.R. Tolkien*

www.ingramcontent.com/pod-product-compliance
Lightning Source LLC
Chambersburg PA
CBHW050517100526
44581CB00001B/7